SIMTOWER™

THE OFFICIAL STRATEGY GUIDE

Now Available

Computer Game Books

The 7th Guest: The Official Strategy Guide
Betrayal at Krondor: The Official Strategy Guide
Computer Adventure Games Secrets
DOOM Battlebook
DOOM II: The Official Strategy Guide
Dracula Unleashed: The Official Strategy Guide & Novel
Front Page Sports Baseball '94: The Official Playbook
King's Quest VII: The Unauthorized Strategy Guide
Lemmings: The Official Companion (with disk)
Master of Orion: The Official Strategy Guide
Microsoft Flight Simulator: The Official Strategy Guide
Microsoft Golf: The Official Strategy Guide
Microsoft Space Simulator: The Official Strategy Guide
Might and Magic Compendium: The Authorized Strategy Guide for Games I, II, III, and IV
Myst: The Official Strategy Guide
Outpost: The Official Strategy Guide
Pagan: Ultima VIII—The Ultimate Strategy Guide
Panzer General: The Official Strategy Guide
Rebel Assault: The Official Insider's Guide
Sherlock Holmes, Consulting Detective: The Unauthorized Strategy Guide
Sid Meier's Civilization, or Rome on 640K a Day
Sid Meier's Colonization: The Official Strategy Guide
SimCity 2000: Power, Politics, and Planning
SimEarth: The Official Strategy Guide
SimFarm Almanac: The Official Guide to SimFarm
SimLife: The Official Strategy Guide
Strike Commander: The Official Strategy Guide and Flight School
Stunt Island: The Official Strategy Guide
SubWar 2050: The Official Strategy Guide
TIE Fighter: The Official Strategy Guide
Ultima: The Avatar Adventures
Ultima VII and Underworld: More Avatar Adventures
Under a Killing Moon: The Official Strategy Guide
Wing Commander I and II: The Ultimate Strategy Guide
X-COM UFO Defense: The Official Strategy Guide
X-Wing: The Official Strategy Guide

How to Order:

For information on quantity discounts contact the publisher: Prima Publishing, P.O. Box 1260BK, Rocklin, CA 95677-1260; (916) 632-4400. On your letterhead include information concerning the intended use of the books and the number of books you wish to purchase. For individual orders, turn to the back of the book for more information.

SimTower™

The Official Strategy Guide

Rick Barba

Foreword by
Yoot Saito

PRIMA PUBLISHING

SECRETS OF THE GAMES™ is a trademark of Prima Publishing, a division of Prima Communications, Inc.

PRIMA™ is a trademark of Prima Publishing, a division of Prima Communications, Inc.

Prima Publishing™ is a trademark of Prima Communications, Inc.

Publisher, Entertainment: Roger Stewart
Managing Editor: Paula Munier Lee
Senior Acquisitions Editor: Hartley G. Lesser
Creative Director, Secrets of the Games: Rusel DeMaria
Project Editors: Brett Skogen and Jennifer Fox
Cover Production Coordinator: Anne Flemke
Copy Editor: Colleen Green
Technical Reviewer: Kirk Lesser
Book Design and Layout: Richard Walker
Cover Design Adaptation: Page Design, Inc.

Important:
Prima Publishing has made every effort to determine that the information contained in this book is accurate. However, the publisher makes no warranty, either express or implied, as to the accuracy, effectiveness, or completeness of the material in this book; nor does the publisher assume liability for damages, either incidental or consequential, that may result from using the information in this book. The publisher cannot provide information regarding game play, hints and strategies, or problems with hardware or software. Questions should be directed to the support numbers provided by the game and device manufacturers in their documentation. Some game tricks require precise timing and may require repeated attempts before the desired result is achieved.

ISBN: 0-7615-0042-1
Library of Congress Catalog Card Number: 94-80093
Printed in the United States of America
95 96 97 98 CWO 10 9 8 7 6 5 4 3 2 1

Table of Contents

Foreword by Yoot Saito

SimTower is an entrance to my Hakoniwa-world.

Hakoniwa is the traditional Japanese art form of creating miniature gardens. Using a box, small plants, some waters, and soil, the artist creates a self-enclosed habitat. Though this form is very static, the creator is stimulated by the instinct to shape a living world.

With *SimTower*, I simply tried to create a Hakoniwa-world with new elements: concrete, glass, steel, and the human being. As in a garden, a tower must have a natural flow. The fundamental principles of Hakoniwa still apply. "Waters" must be channeled. Otherwise, growth is impossible.

Think of this book, then, as an indispensable gardening tool. I've supplied Rick Barba with my own strategies for tower growth and maintenance. Rick also received tips from testing and technical assistance groups at Maxis.

Use your magnification glass frequently. Take a look at each of your Sims. Name them, and monitor their daily lives. They are the "waters" that flow through your tower, giving it life. Understand their needs, and carefully direct their flow throughout your Hakoniwa-world.

Yes, there is a sense of power. You own the building; you are responsible for its harmony and balance. Yet you do not "own" its inhabitants. Your Sims go about their lives, fulfilling their own unpredictable needs. Your Invisible Hand cannot control their activities, only observe and accommodate them.

"Life water" falls. Things happen. This is the law of the *SimTower* world, just as it is so in the real world. This is the philosophy of Hakoniwa art, where waters, regardless of your efforts, will always flow to the lowest level. I look forward to many sequel worlds.

Yoot Saito
January 1995
Tokyo, Japan
E-mail: khc02145@niftyserve.or.jp

Acknowledgments

First and foremost, my thanks go to Yoot Saito for his absorbing game, his eloquent Foreword, and his generous assistance in preparing this book. It was an honor to work with Mr. Saito—and though we've met in cyberspace, I look forward to meeting him in real space someday.

Thanks also to the prompt and helpful *SimTower* crew at Maxis, particularly producer Michael Perry, lead tester Michael Gilmartin, QA Manager Alan Barton, and product manager Julia Hing, who kept everything moving on schedule. Thanks also to Maxis CEO Jeff Braun for the fascinating dinner conversation over sashimi in Las Vegas at the 1995 Winter CES. Listening to Jeff vigorously explore topics ranging from hardware to Huna religions helped me understand why Maxis continues to produce deep, fresh, and entirely unique products such as *SimTower*.

Finally, thanks to the Prima SWAT team who quickly assembled all of my disjointed pieces into a whole book. It's always a pleasure to work with nice people who also happen to be awesomely efficient and professional—people like my project editors Brett Skogen and Jennifer Fox, for example. Thanks to Melinda McRae for her Japanese-to-English translation work. And a special thanks to Prima's resident visionary Hartley Lesser, who proposed the idea for a *SimTower* book in the first place.

Rick Barba
January 1995
Omaha, NE
E-mail: rickbarba@aol.com

Introduction

SimTower: The Official Strategy Guide is my eleventh book for Prima's "Secrets of the Games" series. I must begin by saying this book was the most difficult one thus far to actually start writing. The reason? I couldn't pull myself away from *SimTower: The Software.*

Praising the game that happens to be the subject of this book sounds self-serving, I know. But frankly, my obsession with *SimTower* surprised me. I don't consider myself a "gamer"—the term smacks of nerd, geek, mouse potato, *get a life, man.* Games should be a minor diversion from reality, not a substitute for it, right? Anyway, most software titles (even "open-ended simulations") yield up their secrets after three or four intense days. Then the game grows old, and it's time to write.

But with *SimTower*, I couldn't stop playing, if playing is the correct word to describe the experience.

I spent 12 straight days, staring at my monitor, chewing my cheek, bouncing my knee, totally obsessed with things I never thought I'd care about—elevators, for instance. Had to get up there, man. Get to floor 100. Get that cathedral. Can't sleep. Build. Build more.

My life was progressing in 15-floor intervals.

Oh, I took notes. Here and there. But mostly I just played. When I wasn't playing, I thought about playing. Then I'd go to bed at night and dream about playing.

Maybe you've had a similar experience with *SimTower*. If so, read on. I can help. I've been there, man. That gut-wrenching moment when you realize your Express elevator with its full rack of eight cars—a tidy $1.6 million investment—is badly placed, should be destroyed, rebuilt. Insomnia sets in. Your shops are going out of business. Little red people are queued up, everywhere. You want to call Maxis, call Yoot Saito in Tokyo, get counseling.

That's what I did.

Fortunately, it's my job. The phone calls and psychotherapist bills are tax write-offs. And, you'll be happy to know, both Maxis and Yoot Saito were more than accommodating.

So read on. Let me help solve your *SimTower* anxieties.

Then go get some sleep.

How to Use This Book

First of all, note that this is a strategy guide, not a manual. I've included most of the nuts and bolts of *SimTower* operation, but I've also made many assumptions about your knowledge of the program. For example, this book assumes you bought the software legally and hence, obtained a copy of the *SimTower* User's Manual and actually read it.

So if you're not familiar with at least the rudiments of *SimTower* building, I suggest you first read the excellent Maxis documentation. Then come back to *SimTower*: *The Official Strategy Guide*. You'll find that it's divided into 14 easy-to-use chapters full of strategic overviews, hints, tips, and other information you won't find in the manual.

Such as:

Part 1: Getting Started focuses on the game's interface (windows, menus, buttons, etc) and includes some general information about tower costs, requirements, and limits. This section also introduces you to your "SimFolks" and explains how and why you should track individual Sims.

Part 2: Zoning takes a look at the various types of tenants—office, shop, condo, hotel, entertainment, etc.—and suggests efficient configurations. It also offers proven tips on strategic placement of Security, Medical, Housekeeping, and Recycling centers, as well as Parking facilities and your Metro Station.

Part 3: Transportation examines the critical arteries of your tower—elevators, escalators, and stairs.

Part 4: Pricing, Evaluation, and Special Features discusses how to maximize income while keeping rents and services in line with tenant/visitor expectations. This final part also helps you deal with tower emergencies such as VIP visits, fires, bomb threats, bug infestation and more.

Again, the focus is on strategy. You won't find installation instructions—hey, you got those in the gamebox, didn't you? (Unless you're a pirate.) Nor will you find any of the technical mumbo-jumbo about start-up problems, system errors, memory requirements, boot disks, hardware and software compatibility, or other eerie phenomena. If you're having technical trouble with the

Along the way, you will occasionally see this icon. It signifies that I'm revealing undocumented features or rewards (commonly known as "Easter Eggs") tucked into the program by the designer. One example is the appearance of Santa Claus at the end of each *SimTower* quarter. Some of these features are fleeting, others less transitory in nature. All are fun.

game—if it's crashing, turning odd colors, hissing at you—don't come to me or this book. Go to Maxis. They know everything.

You can reach Maxis Technical Support at (510) 253-3755, Monday through Friday, 8:00 A.M. to 6:00 P.M. (PST). Or you can fax your questions to Maxis at (510) 253-3736, or mail them to Maxis Technical Support, 2 Theatre Square, Orinda, California, 94563-3346. Don't forget the Maxis BBS via modem at (510) 254-3869.

PET
17
15
12
11
10
8
5
4

Part 1

Getting Started

1 SimTower Basics

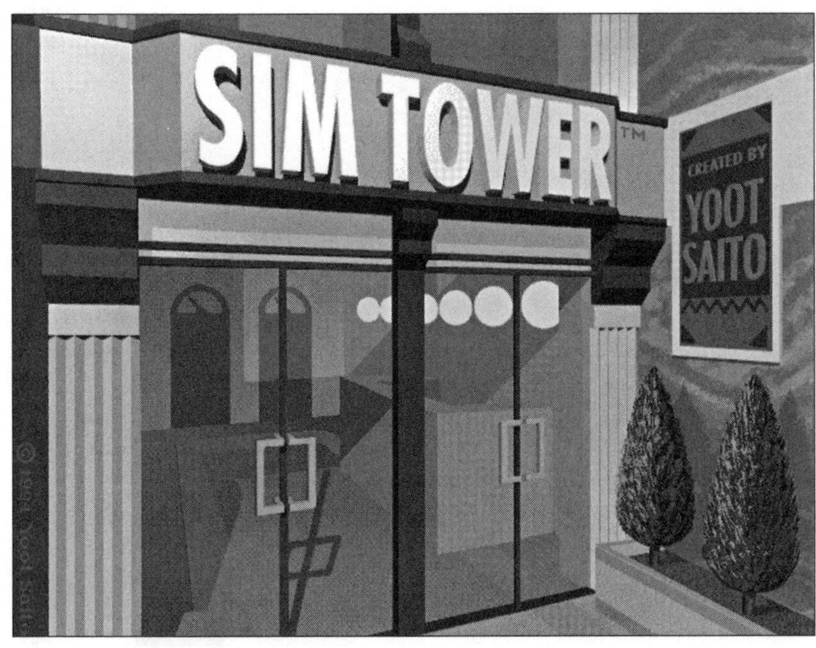

Figure 1-1.
Welcome to Yoot's World.

This opening chapter is a nuts-and-bolts introduction to the basic *SimTower* tools and interface. As such, it's probably geared more toward those of you who are new to *SimTower*. Veteran tower builders should probably skip ahead to Chapter 2—but not before checking out the nifty "kickstart" feature at the end of this chapter.

The SimTower Day

Here's a quick look at your daily schedule. Every *SimTower* day unfolds in the same manner, except that on the Weekend (WE), your Offices remain closed all day.

5:00 A.M.	Dawn
6:30 A.M.	Hotel guests begin to check out (continues until 12:00 P.M.)
7:00 A.M.	Garbage pickup
9:00 A.M.	Workday begins

10:00 A.M.	Shops, Fast Food open
12:00 Noon - 1:00 P.M.	Lunch hour
1:00 - 4:00 P.M.	Movie runs in theaters
5:00 P.M.	Offices begin to close Restaurants open Income from Party Halls
5:00 - 8:00 P.M.	Movie runs in theaters
6:00 P.M.	Dusk
8:00 P.M.	Movie Theaters close Income from Movie Theaters
9:00 P.M.	Shops, Fast Food close Income (loss) from Fast Food
11:00 P.M.	Restaurants close Income (loss) from Restaurants

The Edit Window

Figure 1-2. Edit Window. Come on, build something, will you? I'm getting agoraphobic out here, man.

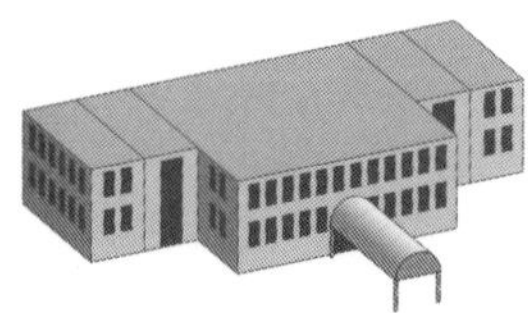

The Edit Window is the show, baby. This is the main display area in *SimTower*, the one where everybody lives and all the fun happens. Zoom it out full screen, shrink it to a puny pixilated cube. Slap a few dozen offices across the top, like icing. Or do nothing. Watch the clouds drift by.

Hey, you read Yoot Saito's Foreword. It's your Hakoniwa. You're the boss.

Of course, you can't do anything in the Edit Window until you learn how to use the Tool Bar. So read on.

The Tool Bar

Figure 1-3. Tool Bar. Belly up to this one. Lots of cool button icons. And a standard VCR-style Pause/Play button at the top.

No, it's not where mechanics drink beer and stuff. It's that small rectangle on the screen (see Figure 1-3), the one full of square icon buttons. These icons are "tools" in every sense of the word. Use them to construct (or deconstruct) your facilities, floor by floor.

The top four icons on the Tool Bar are your Function Tools. These perform specific actions that are described in the next section. The bottom eight icons on the Tool Bar are your Construction Tools. Click and hold on these to access drop-down menus full of other Construction Tool icons, all of which trigger the actual building of your tower's facilities. For a more complete explanation of each tool's function, read on.

Function Tools

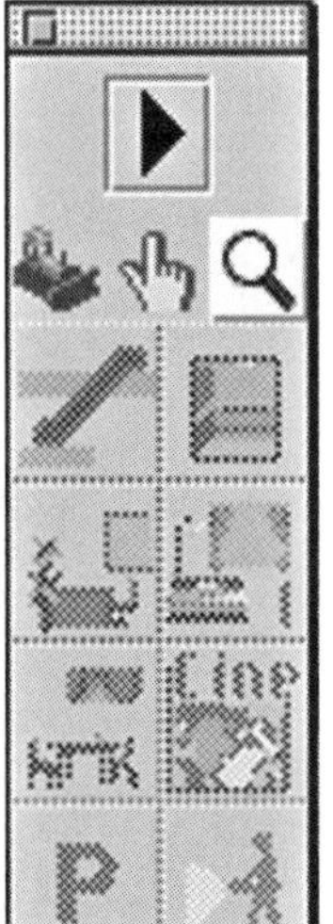

Figure 1-4. Pause/Play Button.

Your Function Tool will perform the following actions.

Pause/Play Button

Those of you familiar with VCR controls (and those of you who aren't, welcome back from your extended coma) will immediately recognize this pair of icons. Click on the Pause button to halt *SimTower*—note that the other Tool Bar icons are disabled, except for the Magnifying Glass (as in Figure 1-4). Click on the Play button to continue.

Bulldozer

Figure 1-5. The Bulldozer.

Turn this guy loose on facilities that offend thee. Also good for clearing fire damage and bomb-blast remnants. Keep in mind that Lobbies, Security, Housekeeping, Recycling Centers, Metro Station, and the Cathedral cannot be bulldozed once they are placed.

Finger

Figure 1-6. The Finger.

A handy little digit. Activate, click, and hold the Finger on the small arrow at the top or bottom of any elevator shaft you wish to extend or contract. Then drag that end of the shaft up or down. The Finger can also suspend floors from elevator service. Just click it on the floor number (which then disappears) on the shaft. To return the floor to service, click on the floor number again.

NOTE The Finger cannot remove "waiting" floors (indicated by pink numbers) from service. You have to first assign the "waiting" cars to another floor. For more on this, see How to Change Waiting Floors in Chapter 11.

Magnifying Glass

Figure 1-7. The Magnifying Glass.

Ultimate spy tool, man. Click on any tower facility to bring up a Facility Window (Figure 1-8). Or click on individual Sims to get a Tenant Window (Figure 1-9) full of intimate details about your selection. The game pauses, and you can check stress levels, adjust rents, and rename your shops, businesses, and people. Take plenty of time to survey your vertical kingdom.

Figure 1-8. Facility Window.

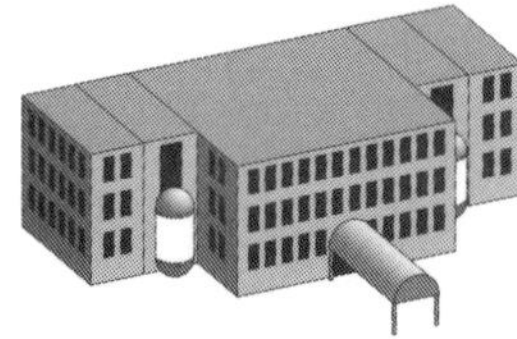

Figure 1-9. Tenant Window.

Construction Tools

Stacked beneath the Function tools are icons that give you access to all 24 types of facilities/services that you can place in your tower. This "access" isn't immediate, of course. Only seven types of facilities are available at first. You add more as your tower's star rating rises.

To activate a tool:

1. Click and hold on the appropriate icon. In most cases, a drop-down menu will appear.
2. Drag the cursor to highlight the tool you want, then release the mouse button. Your cursor will assume the outlined shape of the facility you selected.
3. Move the cursor onto the tower and carefully position it over the area on which you want to construct the item.
4. Now click. The item will be constructed by speedy little workers right before your very eyes.

Lobby Menu

This drop-down menu displays four very important Construction tools—Lobby, Floor, Stairs, and Escalator. For more on these facilities, see Chapters 4 (Lobbies), 5 (Floors), and 11 and 12 (Stairs and Escalators).

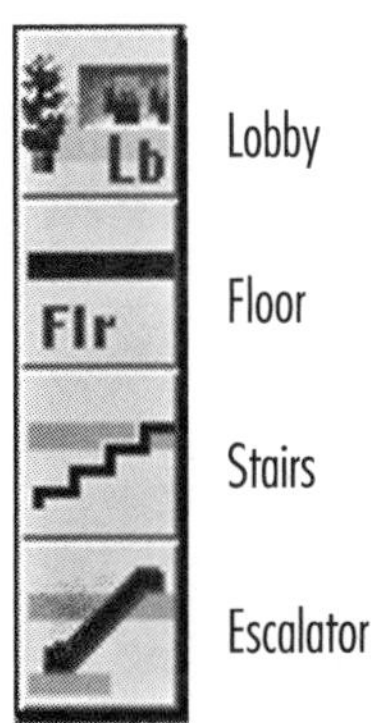

Figure 1-10. Lobby Menu.

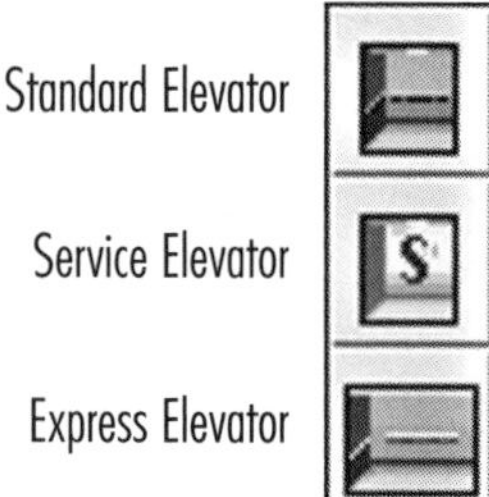

Figure 1-11. Elevator Menu.

Elevator Menu

Vital arteries of your tower. The Elevator drop-down menu displays three types of elevator construction tools—for Standard, Service, and Express elevators. For more on elevators, see Chapters 11 and 12.

Office

Figure 1-12. Office Icon.

Office Icon

Just click on the Office icon. (No drop-down menu here, so a single click activates the tool.) Hey, offices are full of busy people, people who also happen to be voracious consumers. People like you and me. For more info, see Chapter 6.

Housekeeping

Figure 1-13. Hotel Menu.

Hotel Menu

Need daily income? Click and hold on the Hotel icon. A drop-down menu displays hotel construction tools for Single, Twin, and Suite rooms, plus Housekeeping. For more on hotel management, enroll at Cornell University. Or see the Hotel section in Chapter 7.

Condo

Figure 1-14. Condo Icon.

Condo Icon

Need instant income? Click on the Condo icon. Again, there is no drop-down menu. Condos cost $80K to build but can sell for $150-$200K. Tidy profit, eh? For more on Condos, see the Condo section in Chapter 7.

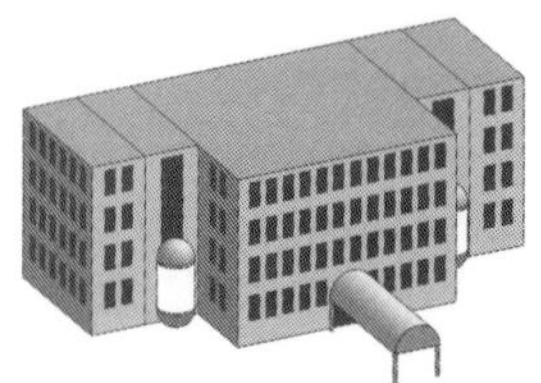

Commercial Menu

Here comes the fun stuff. Shopping! Movies! Party! Financial health and aesthetic diversity both demand a nice assortment of commercial tenants in your tower. For more on developing commercial areas, see Chapter 8.

Figure 1-15. Commercial Menu.

Parking Menu

Indispensable items for towers of substance. Without parking, you're nothing. Also note: When you hit five-star status, you activate the Cathedral tool in this drop-down menu. (We didn't include its icon here, because . . . well, some things should remain sacred.) For more on these crucial infrastructure items, see Chapter 9.

Figure 1-16. Parking Menu.

Security/Medical Facility Menu

Everybody needs Security, especially a Vertical Empire. And before long, your Offices and Condos begin clamoring for Medical Facilities too. Read more about it in Chapter 9.

Security

Medical Facility

Figure 1-17. Security/Medical Facility Menu.

Construction Tool Availability

Again, you start with only seven construction tools, then add others as your tower achieves higher star ratings. The table at left shows which tools become available to you as you reach each star rating level.

Lobby
Floor
Stairs
Standard Elevator
Office
Fast Food
Condo

Service Elevator
Single Hotel Room
Housekeeping
Security

Escalator
Express Elevator
Twin Hotel Room
Hotel Suite
Restaurant
Retail Shop
Cinema
Party Hall
Parking
Parking Ramp
Recycling Center
Medical Facility

Metro Station

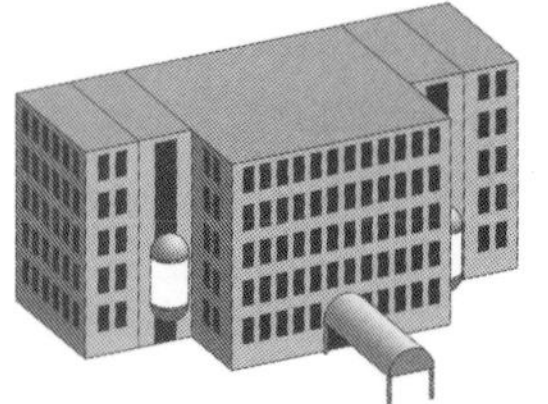

Cathedral

Construction Item Limits

Wouldn't it be cool if (in the spirit of Saturday Night Live) you could build a 100-story tower filled with nothing but Scotch Tape Stores? But alas, no. There are item limits in *SimTower*. Listed below are the maximum numbers of each type of facility you can place in your tower.

Offices	Unlimited
Medical Center	10
Security	10
Elevator Shafts	24
Cars Per Shaft	8
Stairs/Escalator	64 Total
Theater/Party Hall	16 Total
Fast Food/ Restaurant/Shops	512 Total
Parking Spaces	512 Total
Cathedral	1
Metro Station	1

Info Bar

The Info Bar is "data central" of your *SimTower* world. Your user's manual gives you a thorough description of its functions and readouts. But let's review: The game clock at the far left of the Info Bar displays tower time. The stars display your tower's rating. Next to the stars, the date line displays the current *SimTower* day, quarter, and year.

Below that is the message bar, providing pertinent information about item costs, tenant needs, amount and sources of income, and certain special events. ("Santa is coming to your tower!")

Figure 1-18. Info Bar.

Finally, at the far right of the Info Bar are two critical pieces of information. Fund lists your Cash Balance (updated immediately as transactions occur), and Pop displays your tower's current population, including all hotel, restaurant, and shopping visitors, as well as office workers and condo residents.

Map Window

The Map Window lets you see your whole tower at once in a schematic view. There are four buttons at the top of the window labeled Edit, Eval, Pricing, and Hotel. Each one gives you a different set of color-coded information about your tower.

See that small rectangle in the Map Window? It corresponds exactly to the section of tower currently displayed in the Edit Window. (If you resize the Edit Window, that change is mirrored in scale by the map rectangle.) When you move the map rectangle, the Edit Window also scrolls to the new area outlined by the rectangle.

Note also that your elevator shafts are always visible as colored vertical lines in the Map Window—blue for Express, black for Standard, and red for Service.

TIP: In all four Map Window modes—Edit, Eval, Pricing, and Hotel—the Map Window rectangle represents a mini-version of what you see in the Edit Window. Move the rectangle around on the map to quick-scroll the Edit Window view.

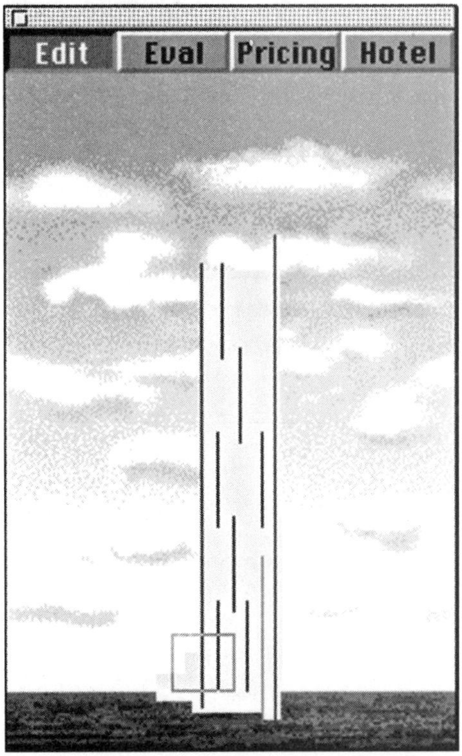

Figure 1-19. Edit Button. In this mode, your tower is a gray silhouette on the map, streaked with elevator shafts—lines of blue (Express), black (Standard), and red (Service).

Edit Button

With the Edit button active in the Map Window (the default choice), you can use the quick-scrolling feature of the map

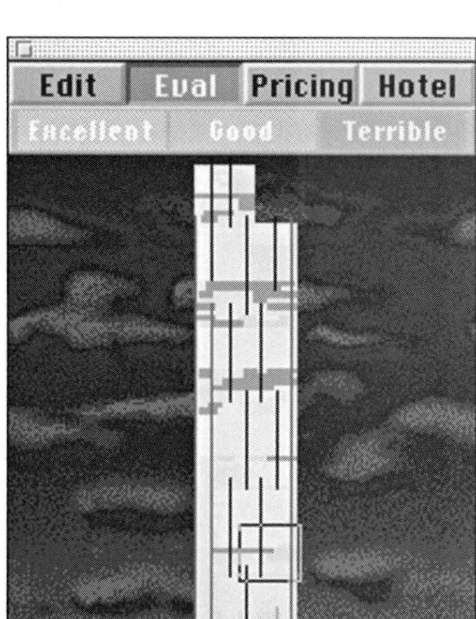

Figure 1-20. Eval Button. This mode pauses *SimTower* and colorfully indicates how tenants rate you as a landlord—Excellent, Good, or Terrible.

rectangle even while the *SimTower* game clock progresses. In Edit mode, you can watch the gray silhouette of your tower sprout up in the Map Window as you add floors, elevators, and other items in the Edit Window.

Eval Button

Click on the Map Window's Eval button to activate *SimTower*'s helpful Evaluation mode. This pauses the *SimTower* clock, and lets you evaluate how you're being rated as a landlord. Ratings are color-coded—blue for Excellent, yellow for Good, and red for Terrible.

Note that the Edit Window close-ups of your properties are also color-coded. Obviously, when you see terrible (red) ratings, you should examine those properties to find out why. Use the Magnifying Glass on all red stuff to open the Facility Window for your selection. Then try to determine just what the heck's bugging these little people.

Pricing Button

The Pricing button helps you keep track of your rent situation. Rental properties are color-coded according to whether they're High (red), Average (yellow), Low (green), or Very Low (blue). These four categories correspond directly to the four levels of rent you can set for each rental property. Pricing color codes appear in both the Map Window and the Edit Window.

Keep in mind that rent levels affect your evaluation levels but not as much as you might think. Tenants paying top dollar can be happy as clams . . . as long as you keep tower traffic flowing, provide good services, and take care of noise and other problems that may crop up.

On the other hand, not even cut-rate rents can compensate for a lousy elevator system.

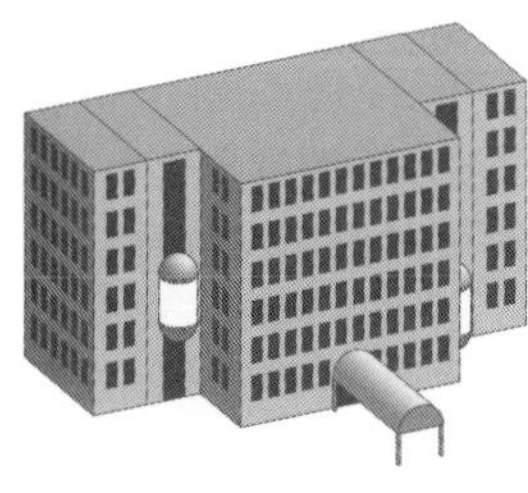

Hotel Button

Bugs? Did you say bugs? What bugs? Hotel bugs, that's what bugs. If you're short on Housekeeping staff, your hotel rooms get

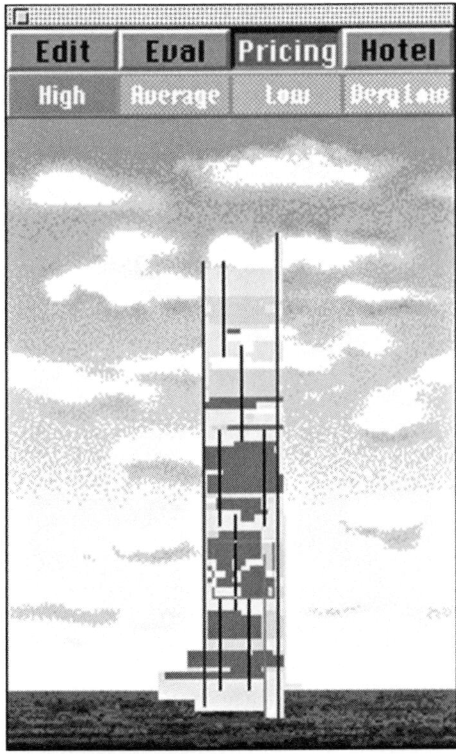

Figure 1-21. Pricing Button.
Are you charging too much rent? Too little? How can you keep track, with hundreds of tenants? Answer: with a handy Pricing button!

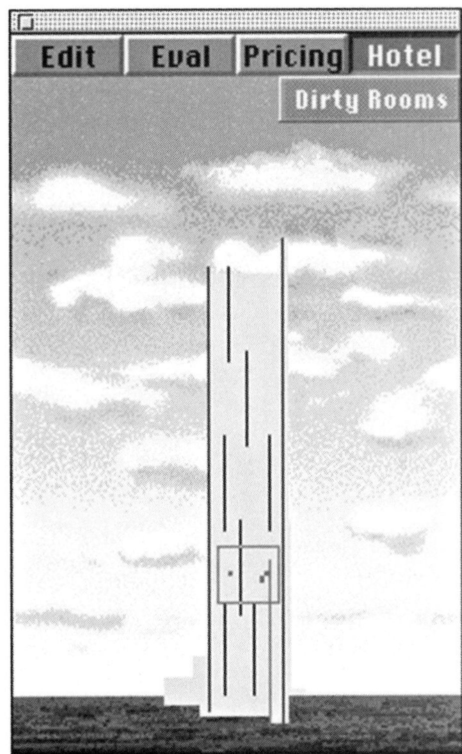

Figure 1-22. Hotel Button.
See those little red dots? Those are dirty hotel rooms, revealed on the Map window by clicking on your Hotel button.

dirty. Dirt leads to bugs, quite quickly. And *SimTower* bugs are the worst—in fact, you'll have to destroy infested rooms. Which costs. So, before any of that happens, you might want to take advantage of the Hotel button in your Map Window. Dirty hotel rooms pop up in red on the map. Then you can marshal your cleaning forces.

Finance Window

There it is. Down there, man. The bottom line. Is your ink black or red? Are you a genius or a megalomaniacal failure?

Your answer is in the Finance Window. Why, exactly, is that important to *SimTower*? Well, I suppose it's kind of interesting to see how things are adding up, see where the real population bulges are. And whoa, look at those Maintenance Expenses. Boy, aren't they something?

Figure 1-23. Finance Window. Net Revenues. Maintenance Expenses. Who cares? You've still got a tower, don't you?

Year 10 Quarter 3

Total Income	Total Maintenance
82530	26070

	Population	Income		Maintenance Expense
Office	1944	36600	Lobby	5870
Single Room	51	2160	Elevator	7700
Twin Room	2	40	Exp Elevator	6800
Hotel Suite	6	60	Ser Elevator	100
Shops	2589	17390	Escalator	2000
Fast Food	1120	1460	Parking Ramp	200
Restaurant	180	280	Recycling Center	2000
Party Hall	50	400	Metro Station	0
Theater	760	1640	Housekeeping	200
Condo	69	22500	Security	1200

(Items with no income or expenses are not displayed)

Net Revenues	56460
Other Income	0
Construction Costs	-129980
Last Quarter's Balance	75409
Total Balance	1889

OK

To be perfectly honest, I opened this window once—during my first tower's first year—then never touched it again. Why do I care about escalator maintenance expenses? Should I care how last quarter's balance stacks up to this quarter's balance?

Answer: I don't know.

Wait. Actually, there is one vaguely useful function for the Finance Window. My technical editor for this book, Kirk Lesser, uses his Finance Window to figure out how many Security, Housekeeping, and Recycling centers he's placed in his tower. He does this by taking the total maintenance expense listed for the item in question, then dividing it by that item's quarterly maintenance rate.

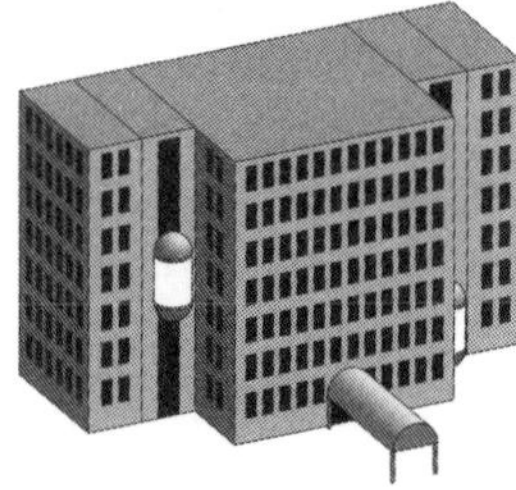

Example: You want to place a Security unit, but you're allotted only ten, so you want to be sure you're not running out. Your Finance Window lists a total Security maintenance expense of $120,000 for the quarter, and you know the per-unit expense is

$20,000 per quarter. So you know you've got six Security facilities in your tower already, with four left to place.

In fact, this is much quicker and easier than scrolling around your tower, trying to pick out and add up the number of Security facilities or whatever. Of course, you could simply note on a handy pad of paper each time you place an item . . . but most of us don't naturally do things like that when we play computer games, do we?

So, here's the glaring hole in this strategy guide. I cannot think of any other good strategic reason for you to consult your Finance Window. If you can, please send the reason via E-Mail to my address—rickbarba@aol.com. I will try to include it in the next printing of *SimTower: The Official Strategy Guide* and will give you direct credit.

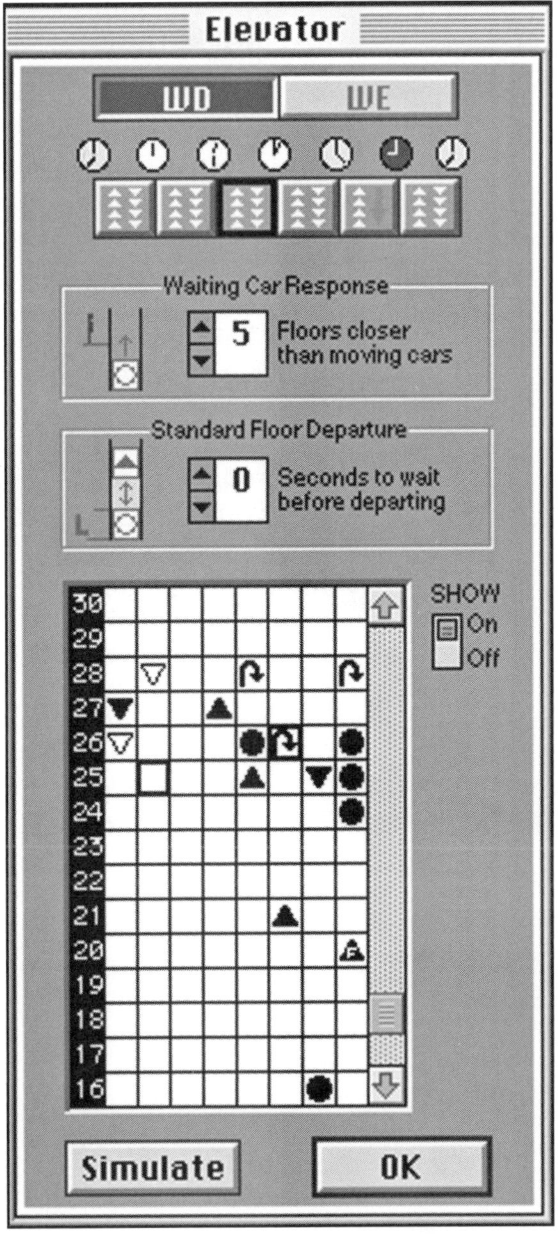

Figure 1-24. Elevator Window. If you really want to get serious about *SimTower,* this is your window, my friend. Do all those tiny little elevator car symbols hurt your eyes? Deal with it.

Elevator Window

Here's where you set your elevator schedules and try to meet those grueling rush hour demands. Unlike the Finance Window, the Elevator Window is something you'll find yourself opening again and again and again. In fact, it's the one you'll probably dream about. This is the heart of the *SimTower* beast.

Each elevator shaft has its own Elevator Window. To access an Elevator Window, simply click the Magnifying Glass anywhere on the visible shaft of the elevator you want. Don't click on elevator cars, though; you'll get a pop-up window for that car, rather than the Elevator Window.

This is all we need to say about the Elevator Window for now. For lots of details and strategies for setting your elevator controls, see the Elevator Window section in Chapter 11.

Star Ratings

Promotions to higher star-ratings require that, in addition to reaching the population marks, you achieve additional milestones. Here's a complete breakdown.

Minimum Population None

Minimum Population 300
Events Terrorist bomb is possible.

Minimum Population 1,000
Requirements More than one security office placed
Events VIP visit, terrorist bomb, and fire are all possible.

Minimum Population 5,000
Requirements Recycling center needed. Tenants demand parking, access to medical center. More than one Hotel Suite room needed, and VIP must have rated your building favorably.
Events Terrorist bomb, fire are possible.

Minimum Population 10,000
Requirements Metro placed; new Recycling and Medical demands met.
Events Fire is possible.

Minimum Population 15,000
Requirement Cathedral placed on 100th floor

Item Costs

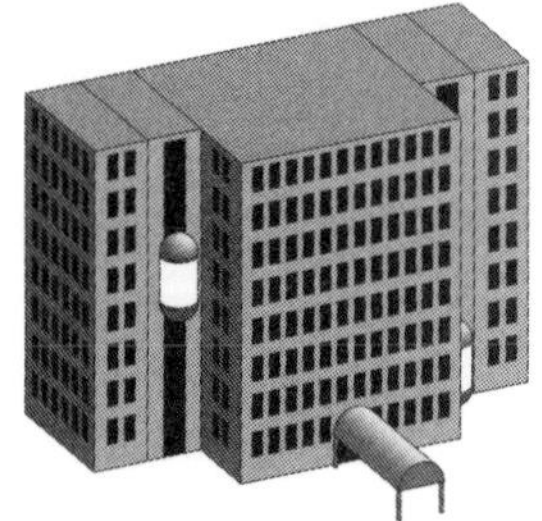

The prices listed in the Cost Chart, on the next page, refer to items placed on an already-built section of floor. But note that in *SimTower*, you often place items where a floor has not yet been built. When this happens, you are automatically charged for the necessary floor sections at a rate of $500 per section.

Cost Chart

Important: Costs listed below do not include the cost of building new floor sections, which are $500 per section.

Item	Cost	Size (# of Floor Sections)	Maint. (Q) (x $100)
Bulldozing	Free	N/A	N/A
Empty Floor	$500 / section	N/A	N/A
Lobbies	$5,000/section	(Lobby Tool = 4 sections)	0/30/100
Escalators	$20,000 ea.	8	100
Stairs	$5,000 ea.	8	0
Standard Elevators	$200,000 ea.	4	100
Service Elevators	$100,000 ea.	4	100
Express Elevators	$400,000 ea.	6	200
Offices	$40,000 ea.	9	0
Fast Food	$100,000 ea.	16	0
Restaurants	$200,000 ea.	24	0
Shops	$100,000 ea.	12	0
Movie Theaters	$500,000 ea.	31 x 2 levels	0
Party Halls	$100,000 ea.	24 x 2 levels	0
Single Hotel Rooms	$20,000 ea.	4	0
Double Hotel Rooms	$50,000 ea.	6	0
Hotel Suites	$100,000 ea.	10	0
Housekeeping	$50,000 ea.	15	100
Condos	$80,000 ea.	16	0
Security	$100,000 ea.	16	200
Medical Center	$500,000 ea.	26	0
Parking Spots	$3,000 ea.	4	0
Parking Gate/Ramps	$50,000 ea.	16	100
Recycling Centers	$500,000 ea.	25 x 2 levels	500
Metro Station	$1,000,000	30 x 3 levels	1,000
Cathedral	$3,000,000	28	0

A Note About Bulldozing Services

Yes, bulldozing services are free. But there is a hidden cost—a rather steep one, at that—when you try to replace Condos. Remember, you actually sold the Condos to little Sim people. Thus, if you choose to bulldoze them, you must buy them back at the original sale price. That's usually about $150,000 a pop.

Also, remember that Lobbies, Security, the Metro Station, the Cathedral, Recycling Centers, and Housekeeping facilities cannot be destroyed (bulldozed) once they are placed.

Kickstart Your Tower

Here's a little cheat function, courtesy of Yoot Saito. To double your startup money from $2 million to $4 million when you begin construction on a new tower, do the following.

1. Boot up *SimTower* and select New Tower.
2. In the Edit Window, scroll your view as far to the bottom and left as possible. (You should be way underground.)
3. Move your cursor into the extreme lower-left corner of the Edit Window.
4. Click the mouse button.

Your opening cash balance will automatically double from $2,000,000 to $4,000,000. Happy Easter.

You get only one chance at this, so be sure you click in the extreme lower-left corner. Once you click on any spot in the Edit Window other than the correct one, you've disabled the "kick-start" function. You'll have to quit the game, then reboot *SimTower* and try again.

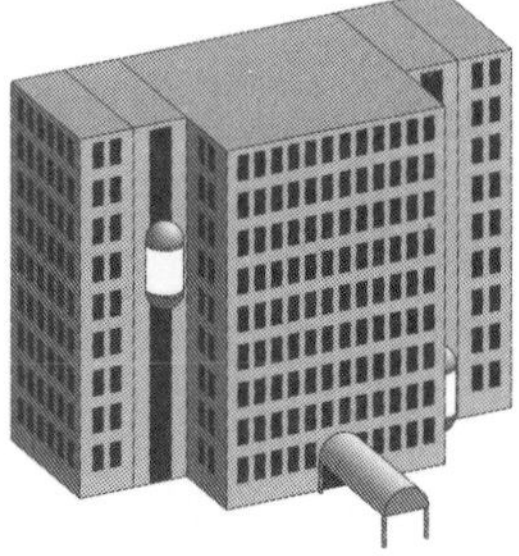

2 SimFaces and SimPlaces

One of the really great things about *SimTower* is the freedom you have to create custom tenants. You can rename every property in your building, thus changing all those dull, generic franchises (Drug Store, Flower Shop, etc.) into unique mom 'n pop shops. Even better, you can root out 20 unsuspecting Sim people, give them individual identities, and track their activities. You get to be the CIA and your suspects pay you rent. Is that a deal, or what?

Meet Your SimFolks

Before we examine *SimTower* structures and strategies and other inhuman phenomena, let's take a moment to acknowledge the little people who've made it all possible. Below is an introduction to the types of Sims who can inhabit your skyscraper.

Man

Yeah, he's a guy. And like most guys, he's nondescript. He's also everywhere. Offices, Condos, Hotels, Shops, Theaters, Restaurants—you name it, they're full of guys. Where do these guys come from? Some scholars have suggested Mars. Others trace their origins to slugs and other sebaceous mollusks.

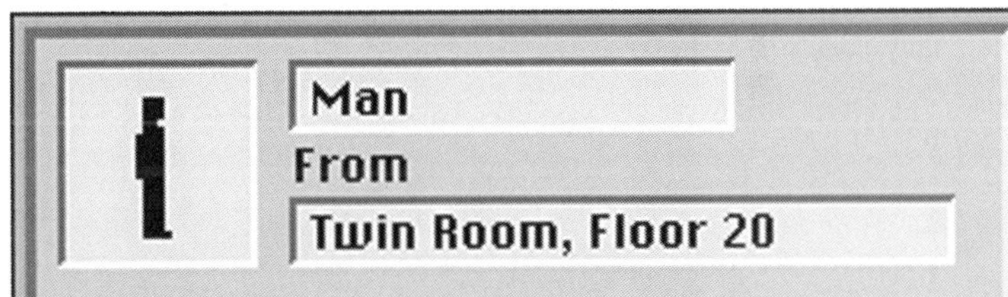

Figure 2-1.
Standard Issue Man.

Woman

Interestingly, there are three different types of female Sims, all simply classified as "Woman." (Guys obviously designed this game.) Two of them, shown here, represent your classic corporate types. You'll find them in almost every Office in your tower. Trim and fierce in their tailored suits, they frequently dine, shop, and mingle with others like them who hail from the Outside.

Figure 2-2. Corporate SimWomen.

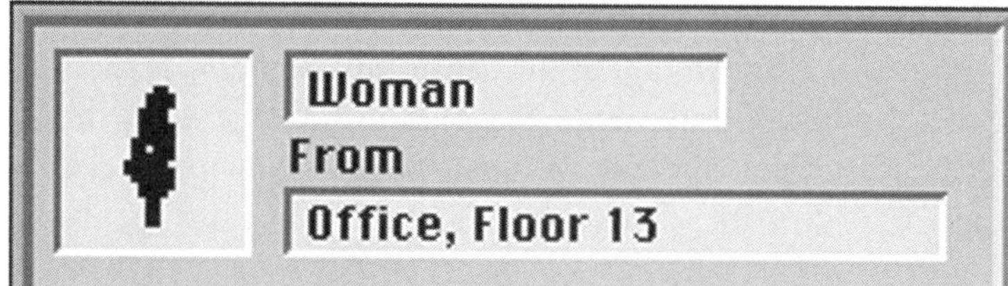

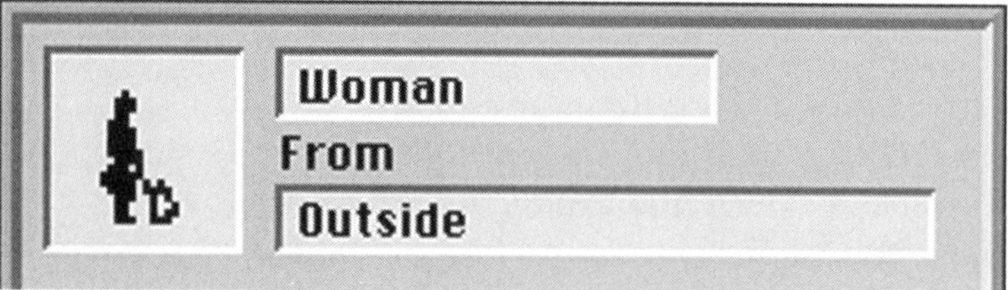

Figure 2-3. SimWoman Who Shops.

Woman (shopping)

At least, I think she's shopping. The pixellated rendering suggests she's got a shopping bag. Or maybe that's a stroller. But if so, why isn't she called "Woman With Stroller"? I laid awake nights pondering this. Finally, I decided to go ahead and label her "SimWoman Who Shops" (though "Dances With Wolves" ran a close second.) Her place of origin is always listed as Outside.

Salesman

Figure 2-4. Salesman.

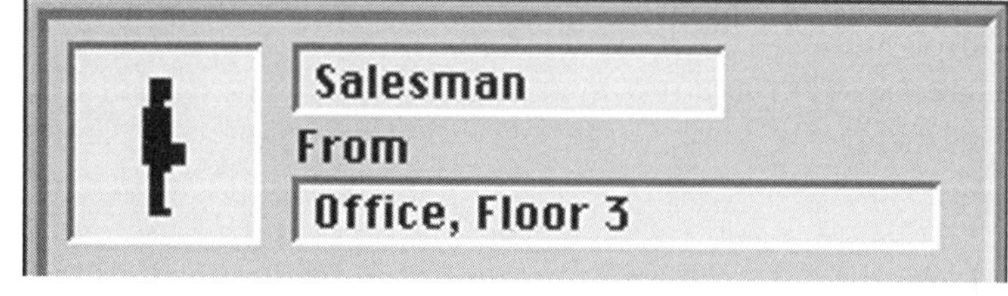

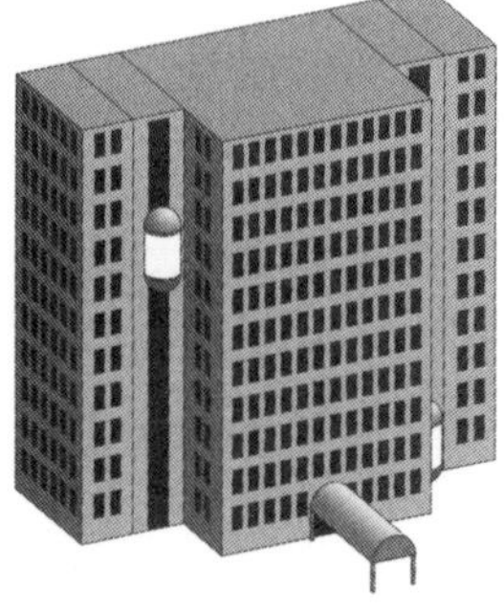

Yes, he is a blockhead with a briefcase. But (to paraphrase Grover Cleveland), the business of *SimTower* is business, and no business is possible without a high-powered sales force. You'll find sales guys jamming into elevators, heading out for sales calls. They also take occasional meals (on the corporate expense account, of course) at your tower food joints.

Child

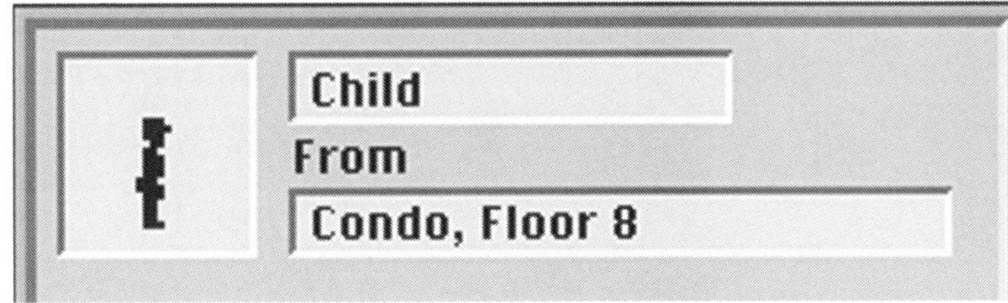

Figure 2-5. Child.

Cute kid. One comes with every Condo, whether you want it or not. He goes to school in the morning, comes home in the evening, then gets out his little red truck. One can only imagine what Junior's day is like—playing, studying phonics, beating up toddlers. Does he have friends? Or has digital tower life so warped him that only modem chat sessions are possible?

Woman With Kid

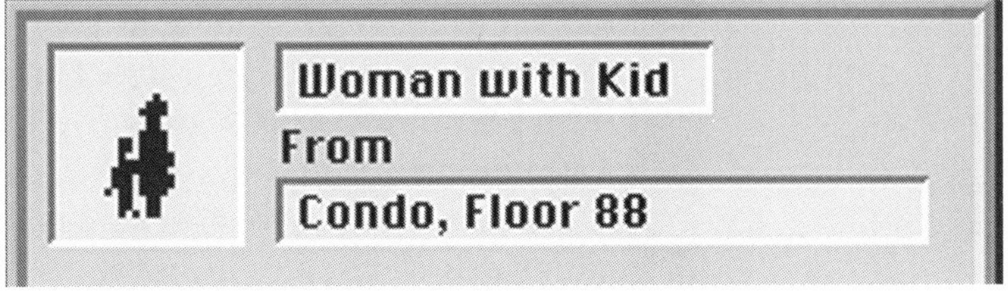

Figure 2-6. Woman With Kid.

Looks like some kind of weird binary species, its two nodes apparently joined at the hip. They travel everywhere like this. Some emerge from Condos on insidious errands. Others infiltrate from Outside. It's frightening, man. I don't know. Maybe I'm paranoid. But my towers are full of them. I can't keep them out!

Housekeeper

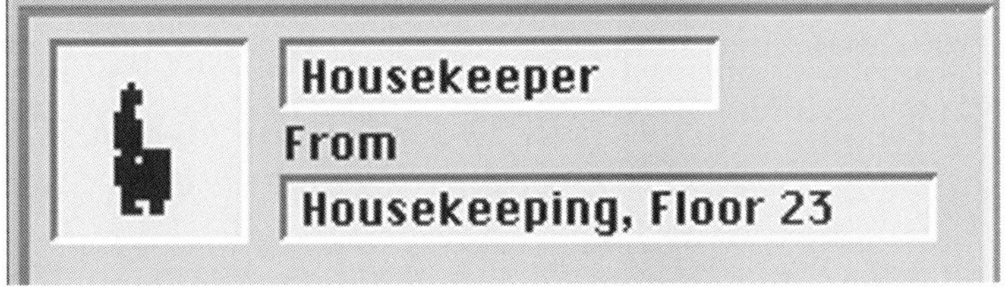

Figure 2-7. Housekeeper.

You'll find six of these burly babes in every Housekeeping Facility. I usually place three or four groups, then name each one of them "Hazel." Here's a strategy tip: Watch them clean for hours, until you go insane. Then seek therapy. It's a pretty good way to change your life.

Security

These come half a dozen per Security Facility. Here's my ad copy for this one: "At *SimTower*, Security is More Than Just a Concept. It's Six Little Guys With Strange Embolic Bulges." I mean, look at the guy. What's going on here? Well, OK . . . he gets the job done by defusing bombs, dousing fires, and stuff. I suppose we should let him carry whatever he wants in his pockets.

Figure 2-8. Security.

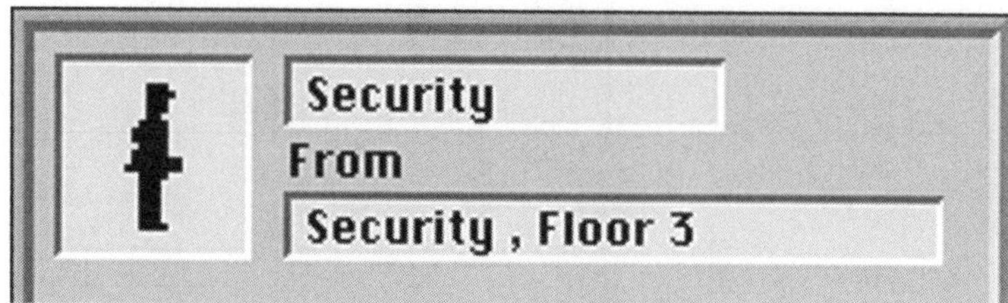

How to Personalize Your Sim People and Properties

SimTower lets you name all of your business offices, shops, restaurants, facilities—everything in your tower, in fact. It also lets you single out up to 20 of your little Sim people, name them, and track them relentlessly. This is great voyeuristic fun, but it can also serve a strategic purpose.

Example: An office area suffers from consistently terrible evaluations. To find out why, name an office in that area, then name one or two of its workers. Now you can track their routes. What tower transportation do they use? What triggers their stress? If you can pinpoint the problem, maybe you can solve it by installing more efficient transport routes, medical facilities, or whatever the little guys seem to need.

To name an individual Sim, you'll need to bring up his/her Tenant Window. There are two ways to do this:

1. If the Sim you want to name is moving through the tower, just click on his/her little body.

   Or . . .

   To name a Sim in a particular facility, first click on that facility to bring up the Facility Window, then click on one of the Sims in the Occupants box (middle-left of window).

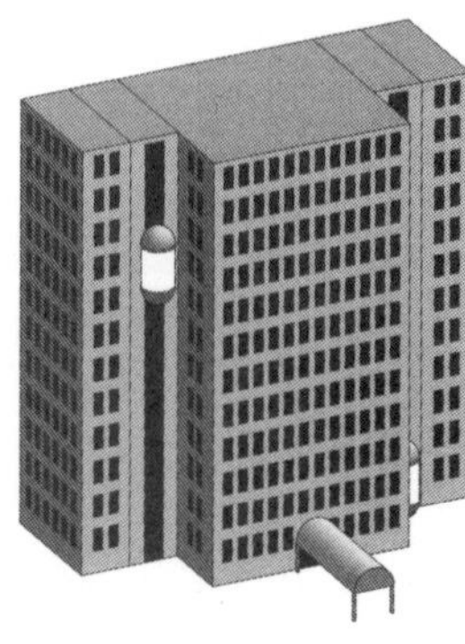

2. When the Tenant Window appears for the selected Sim, click on Rename.
3. Type in a name up to 15 characters long, then click Rename.
4. Click OK.
5. If you picked your Sim from a Facility Window, you'll have to click OK again.

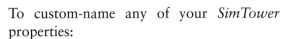

To custom-name any of your *SimTower* properties:

1. Click the Magnifying Glass on the desired property to bring up the Facility Window.
2. Click on Rename.
3. Type in a name up to 15 characters long.
4. Click on Rename again.
5. Click OK.

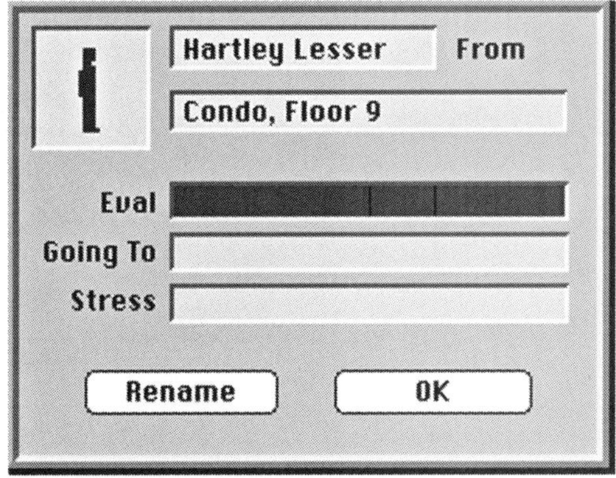

Figure 2-9.
Up Close and Personal.
Get one-on-one with 20 or so of your favorite Sim tenants. Then follow them around like the omniscient narrator of some pitiless Russian novel.

Once you name persons or facilities, you can easily pick them out of your tower's mass mania later. Just select Find Person or Find Tenant from the Windows menu at the top of the screen, highlight your choice, then click on Find. The Edit Window automatically scrolls to your selection, and a convenient red arrow points to the one you seek.

Your personalized Sims actually leave your tower at times. (Hard to believe, isn't it?) When this happens, you are so informed.

Figure 2-10. Name Your Office.
Businesses are drudge buckets unless they sell something cool. (But don't ask me what a "geigger" is.)

Figure 2-11. Let's Find Hartley!
Select Find Person from the Windows menu at the top of the screen, highlight the person you want in your list of named Sims, then click on Find.

Figure 2-12. No Escape for Hartley.
SimTower now scrolls your Edit Window right to Hartley's hide-out. See the big red arrow? That's your guy

PET
PET
74
73
72
69

Part 2

Zoning

How to Create an Efficient Tower

PET
PET
74
73
72
69

3 What is Zoning?

With *SimTower*, it is best to construct "zoned" towers—that is, towers that house certain types of properties clustered in specific areas. Part 2 of *SimTower: The Official Strategy Guide* examines each particular type of property and suggests efficient configurations. But let's start with more general considerations.

Successful *SimTower* developers tend to work from a master plan. I know . . . you're thinking, "Look what master planning did for the Soviet Union." But it doesn't have to be a strict blueprint. You can be flexible and creative and laissez faire in your tower-building. You can have fun. All I'm saying is, don't just throw stuff on the screen. Be patient. Think ahead.

Planning is particularly important when you place elevator shafts. In general, keep your tower's "skeleton" of infrastructure

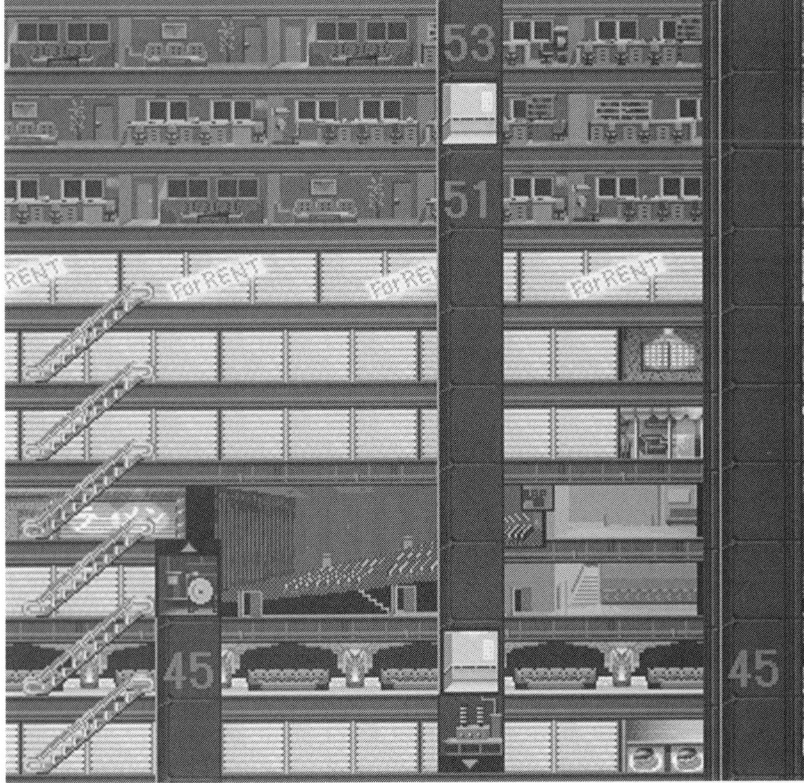

Figure 3-1. In the Zone. A well-zoned area can be a thing of beauty—balanced, harmonious, self-sufficient. And profitable.

(transportation, waste removal, security, medical facilities, etc.) strong, well-balanced, and a step ahead of your rental property development. In the long run, you'll save a lot of time and money. You'll lose few, if any, tenants.

To understand why zoning is the best strategy, you need to understand how the *SimTower* transportation system works. You'll learn everything you need to know about that in Part 3. However, for the sake of general zoning strategy, keep in mind the two fundamental transport rules of *SimTower*: (1) Sims transfer from elevator to elevator only on Sky Lobby floors, and (2) Sims change elevators only once per tower journey.

For zoning to be effective, then, you need to do the following:

- Build a Sky Lobby every 15 floors — that is, on floors 15, 30, 45, 60, 75, and 90.
- Use Standard elevators to connect the 16-floor segments, running from one Sky Lobby to (and including) the next Sky Lobby.
- Run Express elevators to the top of the building.

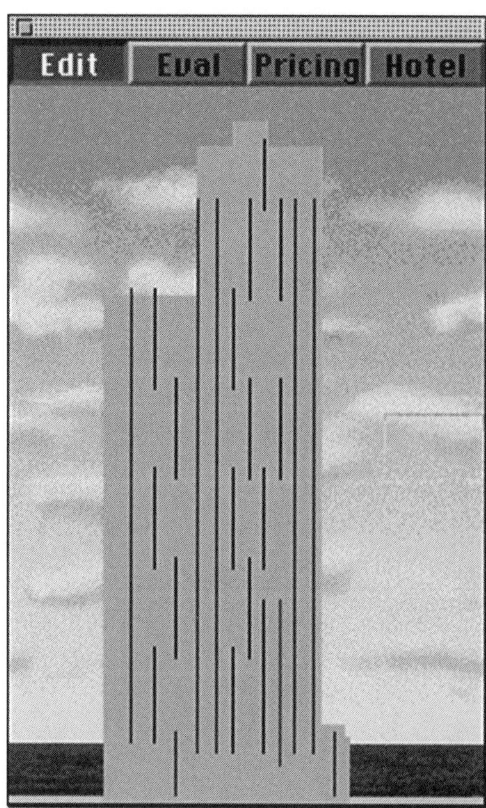

Figure 3-2. Zone Infrastructure. Here's a map depicting the infrastructure of a well-zoned tower. Note that every 15 floors, a phalanx of overlapping Standard elevators flanked by Express elevators appear, connecting the Sky Lobbies.

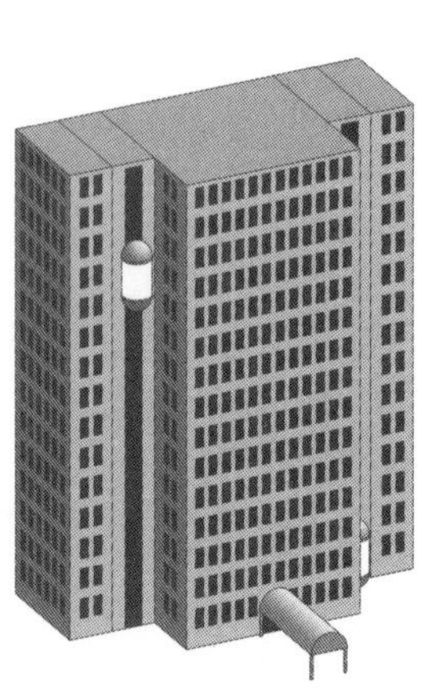

Without Express elevators, your Sims cannot take the elevator above the fifty-ninth floor. Why? Again, only one elevator transfer is possible, and Standard elevators are limited to 30 floors. So Sims can take one Standard elevator from ground level up to a thirtieth-floor Sky Lobby, transfer to another Standard elevator running 30 more floors (30 to 59), and that is it. No more transfers. Stuck.

Zoning and The Ultimate Goal

Maxis refers to *SimTower* as an "open-ended simulation"—meaning, of course, that you do not "win the game" but rather follow any one of an infinite number of paths to a self-defined "conclusion." However, as Maxis lead tester Michael Gilmartin explained in one of our conversations, "Really, your ultimate goal is to build a massive, self-sufficient tower."

Of course, he's right. Once you get there, you'll know what he means. It's not quite enough to merely attain a Tower rating. Somehow, your construction efforts are incomplete if you can't walk away from *SimTower* for awhile without returning to face a sea of red—failing tenants, angry tenants, or already-vacated tenants.

So before we move on to the particulars of tower zoning, let me reiterate its crucial importance. As any tower approaches the 100-story mark and grows in density of population, *SimTower's* limits on transportation devices place a tremendous strain on your transit grid. (Remember, only 24 elevator shafts and a combination of 64 elevators and staircases can be built.) These limits ensure that even the most efficient transit system will fail eventually unless you've zoned your tower properly.

In short, zoning maximizes the efficiency of your transit system. You simply cannot construct a massive and self-sufficient tower without creating separate commercial, office, and hotel zones.

PET
PET
74
73
72
69

4 Lobbies

Lobbies are your *SimTower* launching pads. As connecting points for your elevator system, they serve as the platforms from which your SimFolk skyrocket to their higher destinations. Since Sims can transfer elevators only on lobby floors, lobby placement is a very, very important part of *SimTower* strategy.

Figure 4-1.
Get in on the Ground Floor.
You can't get anywhere in SimTower without first laying a ground-floor lobby.

General Strategy

Fortunately, lobby placement is also a very simple part of *SimTower* strategy. All you have to do, lobby-wise, is lay a ground-floor lobby, then make sure to put another one (called a Sky Lobby) every 15 floors—that is, on floors 15, 30, 45, 60, 75, and 90. That's it for lobby strategy.

Keep in mind that a lobby is a "draggable" feature—you don't have to build it block by block. Simply click and hold the Lobby tool cursor on one end of the proposed lobby, then drag it straight across to the other end, and release. Also, remember that you cannot remove a lobby once it is placed. (Not that you would ever want to.)

Figure 4-2. What a Drag. I mean that in a good sense. Dragging lobbies across the screen is fun and oh-so-expeditious. (If you're wondering why this lobby-in-construction is three stories tall, read on.

Always build a Sky Lobby every 15 floors. Otherwise, your Sims cannot transfer from elevator to elevator.

Sky Lobbies

As mentioned earlier, it is absolutely essential that you build Sky Lobbies on floors 15, 30, 45, 60, 75, and 90. Without Sky Lobbies, your Sims are unable to transfer elevators. Also note that on a Sky Lobby floor, the lobby must extend all the way from elevator shaft to elevator shaft. Even a single section of open floor between elevators prevents Sims from making the transfer.

But here's a money-saving tip: The lobby doesn't have to extend *behind* the elevator shaft. All it has to do is touch the edge of it! (For an illustration of this, see Figures 4-3 and 4-4.) So don't build sections of Sky Lobby in the spaces where elevator shafts cross a lobby—leave the floor open!

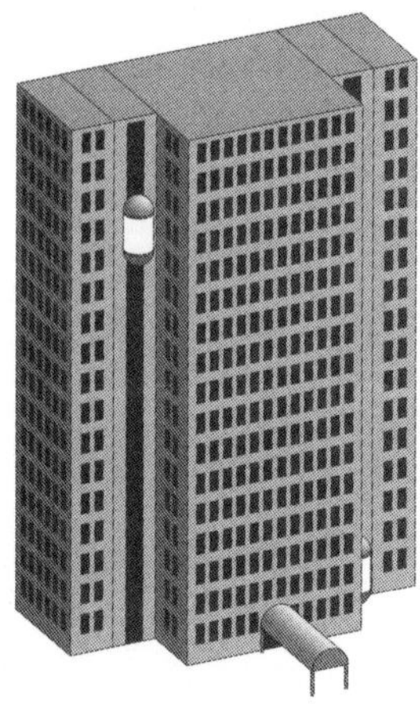

Eventually, this tip can save you hundreds of thousands of dollars. Remember, every section of lobby costs $5,000. Standard and Service elevator shafts are four sections wide, so putting a Sky Lobby in the space behind each one costs $20,000 apiece. With Express elevators (six sections wide), the cost climbs to $30,000. In a 100-story tower, your elevator shafts stop at or cross Sky Lobbies 50 to 75 times. That's a lot of money saved.

Rest assured that an open-floor gap in the Sky Lobby behind an elevator does not prevent Sims from transferring to other elevators further down the floor, either. Once your lobby touches the edge of the elevator shaft, *SimTower* recognizes the whole area behind the shaft as a constructed lobby.

Figure 4-3. Sky Lobby. Build Sky Lobbies every 15 floors and be sure they reach all the way to your elevators. In this shot, Sims make an elevator transfer on the Floor 15 Sky Lobby.

Figure 4-4. However, the lobby doesn't have to fill in the area behind the elevators (as shown here) to connect them.

TIP Sky Lobbies only need to touch the edges of neighboring elevator shafts to connect them for transfer. To save money, don't build sections of Sky Lobby in the space behind elevator shafts—leave the floor open!

Lobby Prices

Lobby costs can be confusing. When you click on the Lobby tool, the Lobby price is listed as $5,000 in the Info Bar. This actually represents a "per floor section" price. The Lobby tool, you'll notice, consists of a four-section-wide block. So when you place it and click, you're actually building four sections of Lobby at a time, at $5,000 apiece. That's $20,000, cash.

However, after that first block is built, you can add one-section segments of Lobby, if you desire. Simply place the Lobby tool over an already-built section of the lobby you want to expand. Slide it sideways until only one section of the tool's outline extends past the existing lobby to open space, then click.

Figure 4-5. Truth in Advertising? Don't be misled by this "info" from the Info Bar. Each square block of Lobby constructed in this manner actually costs $20,000.

Ground Level Lobby	=	$5,000 per section (floor is free)
Sky Lobby	=	$5,000 per section (plus floor cost of $500 per section)
Lobby Tool (4-section block)	=	$20,000 (Sky Lobby includes $2,000 total floor cost)

Super Lobbies

You may have noticed that your lobbies grow more lavish as you raise your tower's star rating. But you can actually kick off construction with one of two different "Super Lobbies" on the first floor—a two-story version or a three-story version. These Super Lobbies are not only big and beautiful, they also reduce tenant stress. Apparently, waiting for an elevator is much less unpleasant when you've got a lot of neat stuff at which to stare.

One other cool Super Lobby feature is that stairs placed on both two-story and three-story versions turn into beautiful spiral staircases. (See the examples in Figures 4-6 and 4-7.)

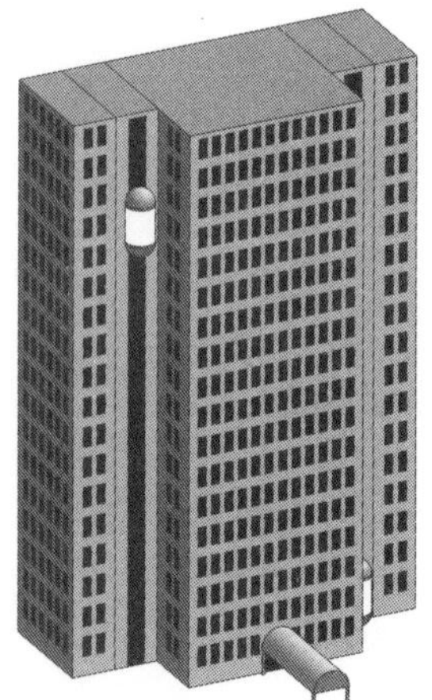

TIP For happier Sims, hold down the Shift-Option keys, then use your Lobby tool to build a three-story lobby on the ground floor. The amount of Sim "waiting" stress decreases with the size of the lobby.

Double Lobby (Ground Level Only)

To build a two-level lobby on the first floor:

1. Boot the game and select New Tower. (If *SimTower* is already booted, select New from the File pull-down menu.)
2. Mac Users: Hold down the Option key.
   PC Users: Hold down the Ctrl key.

3. While holding down the appropriate key (as indicated in step #2, above), click on the place in the Edit Window where you want to construct your first-floor lobby.

Figure 4-6.
Double Your Pleasure.
Yes, you too can build a gorgeous two-level lobby on your ground floor. Note the winding staircase.

Triple Lobby (Ground Level Floor Only)

To build a three-level lobby on the first floor:

1. Boot the game and select New Tower. (If *SimTower* is already booted, select New from the File pull-down menu.)
2. Mac Users: Hold down the Shift-Option keys.
   PC Users: Hold down the Shift-Ctrl keys.
3. While holding down the appropriate keys (as indicated in step #2, above), click on the place in the Edit Window where you want to construct your first-floor lobby.

Figure 4-7. Triple Delight. This stunning three-level lobby on the ground floor can be all yours, too.

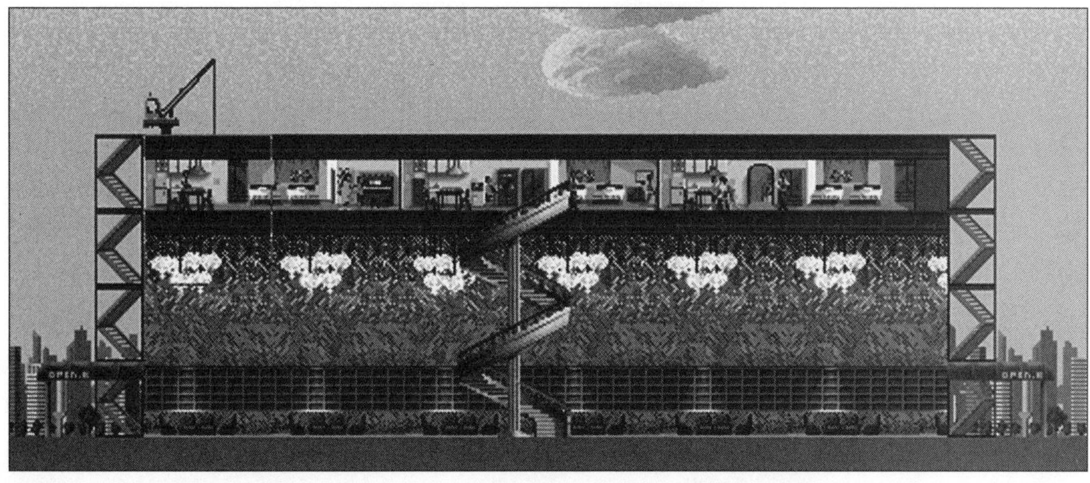

PET
PET
74
73
72
69

5 Floors

Tower facilities don't always layer perfectly. And let's face it, irregular, jagged-edged towers are ugly. Passing pedestrians smirk, whap other people on the shoulder, point up, then everybody falls down laughing. City fathers hate it when that happens. So does any self-respecting tower architect.

Figure 5-1. Smooth Face. Your Floor tool offers a nice, cheap way to eliminate those unsightly jagged edges from your tower. Don't get carried away, though. Remember: Empty floors pay no rent.

So fire up your Floor tool and fill in unsightly overlaps/underlaps with open floor space. Since no floor can exceed the width of the floor just below, it's probably a good idea to smooth off edges. Otherwise, successive stories become narrower and narrower until you run out of working space. Sometimes, though, one can't resist the temptation to stack up empty floors—a quick, cheap way to get a really tall tower and to impress all the people you're dating.

Fine. But remember, empty floor space isn't free.

Floor Costs

In fact, at $500 per thin section, floors can eat up a cash balance faster than you might think. More importantly, empty floors pay no rent. It may not always be worth the cost to simply fill up space with open floor for the sake of aesthetics. And it's hardly a good idea to build a big, tall, empty structure when you could spend that money on construction of properties full of tenants—tenants who increase your tower population and pay cold, hard cash into your coffers daily or quarterly.

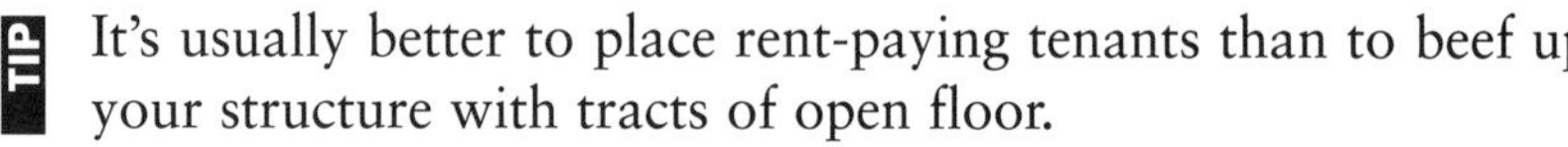
TIP It's usually better to place rent-paying tenants than to beef up your structure with tracts of open floor.

Floors and Zone Jumping

Sometimes, however, it can be smart to lay empty floor space, then develop areas a bit higher up in your tower. Example: It's late in the quarter—any time after 1:00 P.M. on the second Weekday (2nd WD)—and you find yourself with plenty of extra cash. The lower part of your tower is packed full of tenants. At the top,

Figure 5-2. Zone Jumping for Fun and Profit. Occasionally, it's good to lay some open floor, develop a higher area, then work back down.

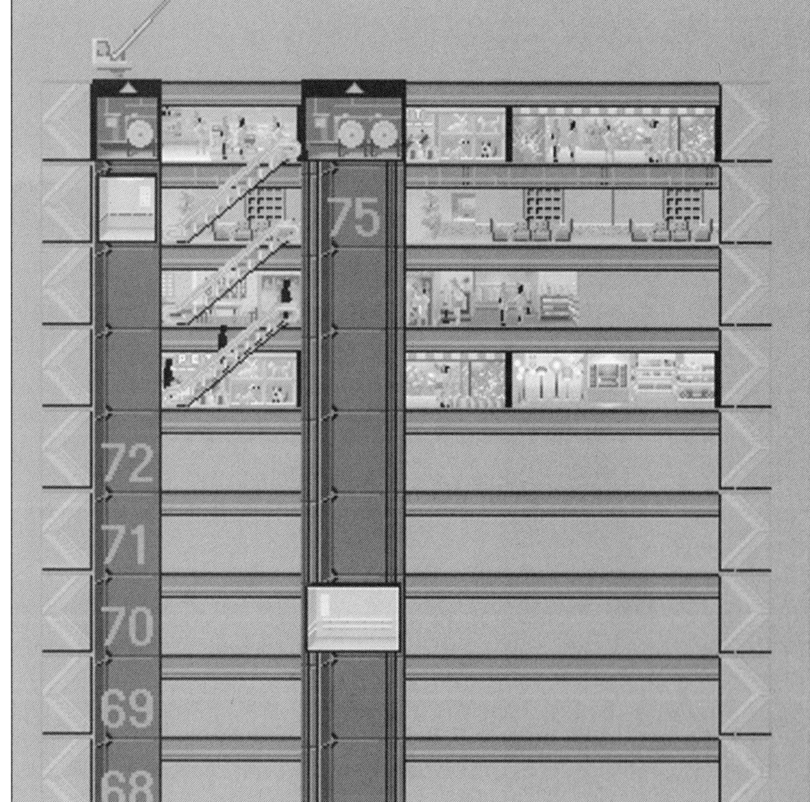

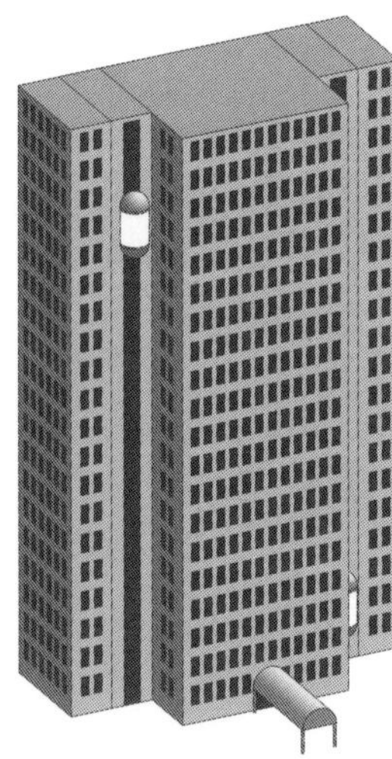

you're in the midst of developing an area you've zoned for offices. (For more on this, see Chapter 6, Office Areas.)

You don't want to build more offices right now though, because offices do not open after 1:00 P.M. on a business workday, nor do they open at all during a weekend. Any office built now will just sit there, unused, until the next quarter begins.

What to do?

One answer is to do a little "zone jumping."

Stack empty floors up to the next new Sky Lobby (the next floor that's a multiple of 15), then develop a shopping zone around it. Why? Because shops open on the weekend. You can collect rent when they open, then collect again the next day (1st WD) when the new quarter begins! Thus, using open floors to "jump up" a zone from office area to commercial area lets you collect double rents.

PET
74
73
72
69

6 Office Areas

The Office is the basic building block of any truly huge tower. Office tenants provide quarterly rental income, of course, but they can also provide a vast pool of customers for your commercial tenants. Office workers are hungry, acquisitive, and restless. They have banking needs. Best of all, the supply of office workers is endless. There is no limit to the number of Offices you can place in your tower.

Each Office can hold up to six workers. Each worker arrives in the morning, eats lunch around noon, then leaves after 5:00 P.M. A few workaholics keep their office lights burning, sometimes well past 8:00 P.M.

Office rents range from $15,000 per quarter at the high end, to $4,000 per quarter at the low end. The default is $10,000 per quarter. Naturally, the lower the rent, the more easily satisfied the tenant. (For 15 grand a quarter, you wouldn't put up with long waits in elevator lines, either.) With Office tenants, it's usually OK to charge premium rents right away, as long as your tower transportation is well developed.

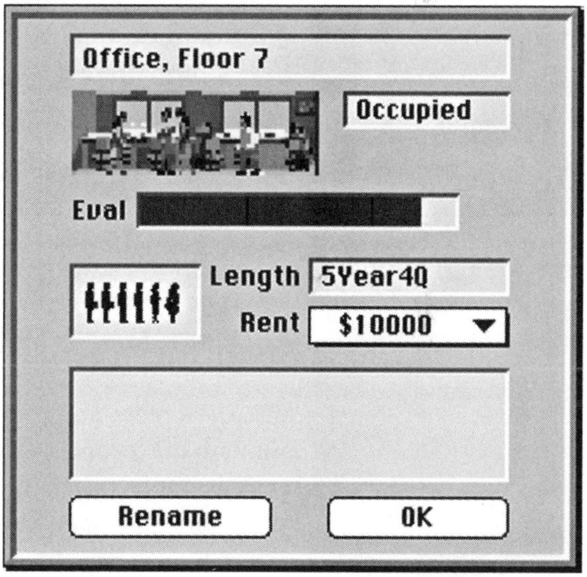

Office, Floor 7
Occupied
Eval
Length 5Year4Q
Rent $10000
Rename
OK

Figure 6-1. Office. This is it—the basic building block of *SimTower* and American civilization. This office is fully staffed, with six workers.

Zoning an Office Area

Commercial tenants, such as retail shops, food outlets, and movie theaters, rely on their proximity to Sky Lobbies for customer traffic. Offices, on the other hand, can thrive anywhere in the tower where there's decent elevator service. In general, then, the idea is to create commercial zones within five floors of your Sky Lobbies, then to fill the remaining areas in between with Offices.

For an example of this basic strategy, take a look at the zoning in Figure 6-2 below.

Figure 6-2.
Zoning Harmony.

Here's a classic zoning strategy. Shops, food outlets, and movie theaters cluster within five stories of the Sky Lobby on Floor 60. An all-Office area rises upward from floor 66.

Note how the Standard elevator (far left) skips commercial floors (61-65), because they're accessible from the Sky Lobby via the system of escalators (center). Office workers can ride the elevator down to the Sky Lobby, then ride escalators up to their shopping/dining destinations. Fewer elevator stops mean speedier service.

Sims from outside the tower can reach both commercial and office zones by taking the Express elevator (far right) to the 60th floor. They can then ride either the Standard elevator to offices or ride escalators to shops and entertainment.

When to Place Offices

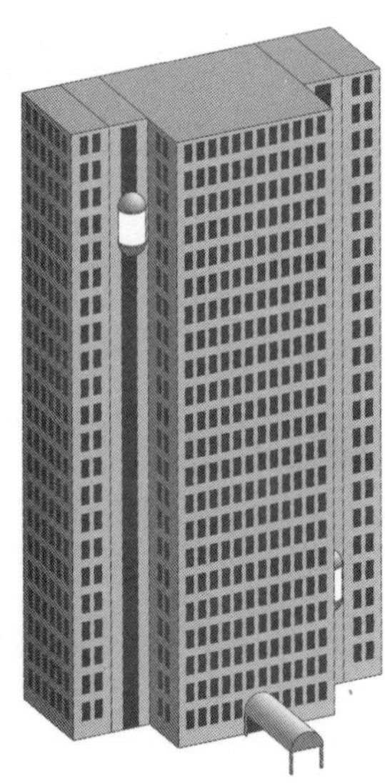

When you place an Office, you receive the first rent payment at the moment the property is first rented. From that point forward, rental income from your Office tenants is added to your Cash Balance at 5:00 A.M. on the first business workday (1st WD) of each new quarter.

Any Office built before 1:00 P.M. on a business workday will find a renter almost immediately if it is connected to the ground floor by transportation. If you build after 1:00 P.M. however, the Office won't open until the morning of the next business workday. (Offices are closed on weekends.)

Hence, it's best to build Offices before 1:00 P.M. on the second business workday (2nd WD) of the quarter. That way, you collect rent when it opens, then collect again with the new quarter. If you build an Office after 1:00 P.M. on the second business workday (2nd WD), it remains unoccupied (and thus, you receive no rent) until the new quarter begins.

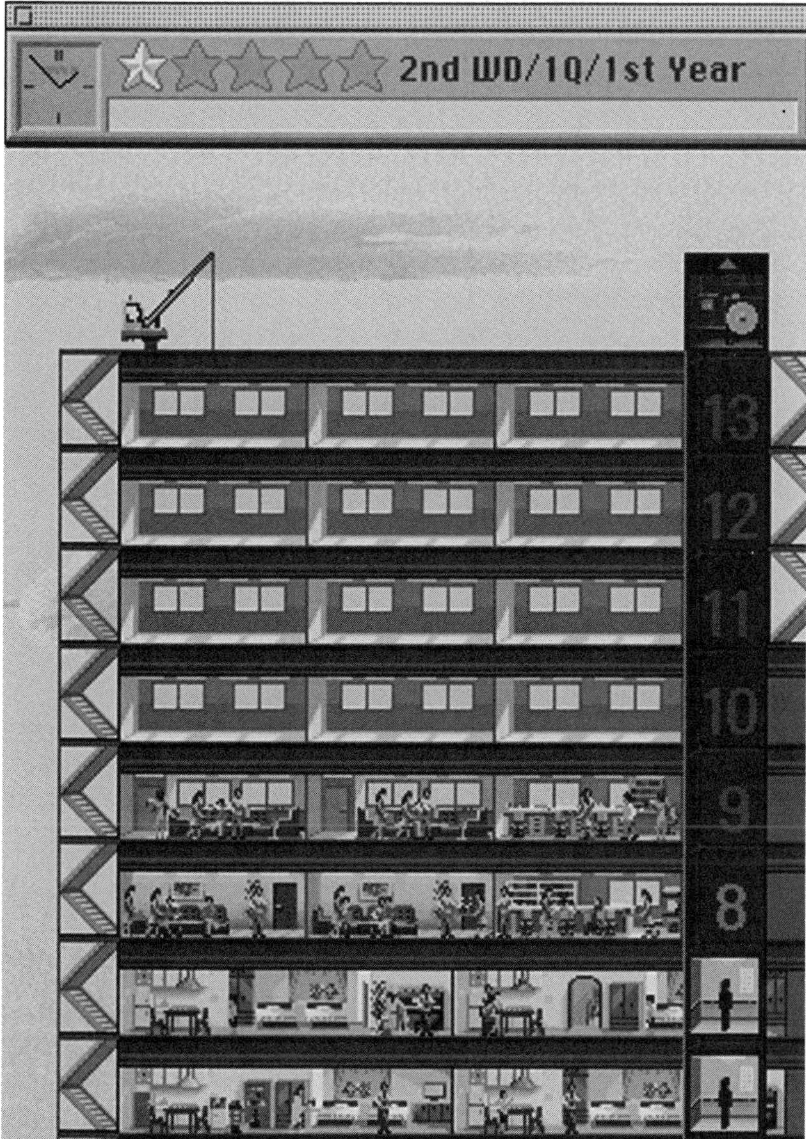

Figure 6-3. Bad Timing. Smart office developers don't do what I did here—build offices after 1:00 P.M. on the second business workday (2nd WD). These top four floors will now remain empty through the weekend.

$15000
✓$10000
$5000
$2000

Figure 6-4. Office Rent. Here's the range of rents you can charge for your *SimTower* Offices. Remember: The more you charge, the less frustration your tenant tolerates.

TIP Try to build Offices before 1:00 P.M. on the second business workday (2nd WD) of each quarter. If you miss that deadline, focus on building other types of properties until the next quarter begins.

Office Noise Problems

Office tenants are sensitive to noise from certain types of neighbors. They don't mind Hotel rooms or Condos next door (though Hotel or Condo occupants aren't too tolerant in return). But if you put any type of commercial tenant—retail shops, fast food, cinema, or other entertainment—on the same floor, office workers complain about noise unless there are at least 11 sections of floor space between their office and the noise source.

Figure 6-5.
Noise Buffer for Offices.
To keep Offices from complaining about noisy commercial neighbors, keep them separated by a space of at least 11 floor sections (as seen here). If you don't . . .

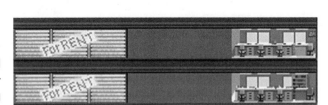

Figure 6-6.
. . . you'll have to deal with irate office supervisors who pull up stakes and leave if the situation doesn't change.

TIP To minimize noise problems for your Office workers, build Office-only floors.

Office Worker Habits

All those corporate lackeys in your *SimTower* high-rise have it made. Everything they could possibly need is just an elevator or two away. Of course, sometimes it's fun to venture out into the city jungle, seeking out luncheon encounters of the urban kind. About

60-70 percent of your office workers dine in the tower on each business workday, if you have enough food joints to accomodate them. The remaining seek culinary variety outside the tower.

By the way, when you click on a Sim and the Tenant Window lists his/her destination as "Going To: Lobby for [whatever]" (as in Figure 6-7), remember that this is *SimTower's* euphemism for leaving the tower.

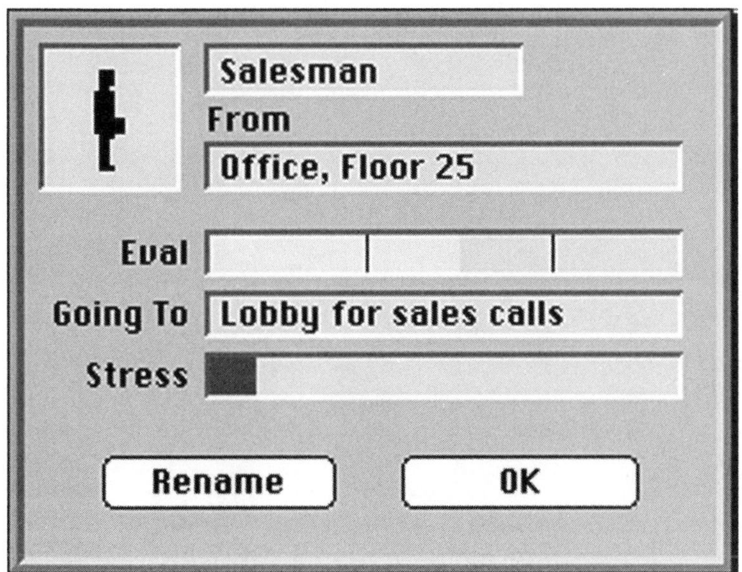

Figure 6-7.
Man on a Mission.
No, this guy doesn't make his sales calls in the lobby. He's actually heading out into the cold, cruel, non-tower world to seek his sales prey.

PET
PET
74
73
72
69

7 Residential Areas

If you wish, your *SimTower* edifice can be a single-minded monument to commerce. But if variety is the spice of life, then *SimTower* offers you a veritable spice-rack of choices for your vertical community. Residential units provide different types of investments. They diversify not only the look of your tower, but also the flow of your income.

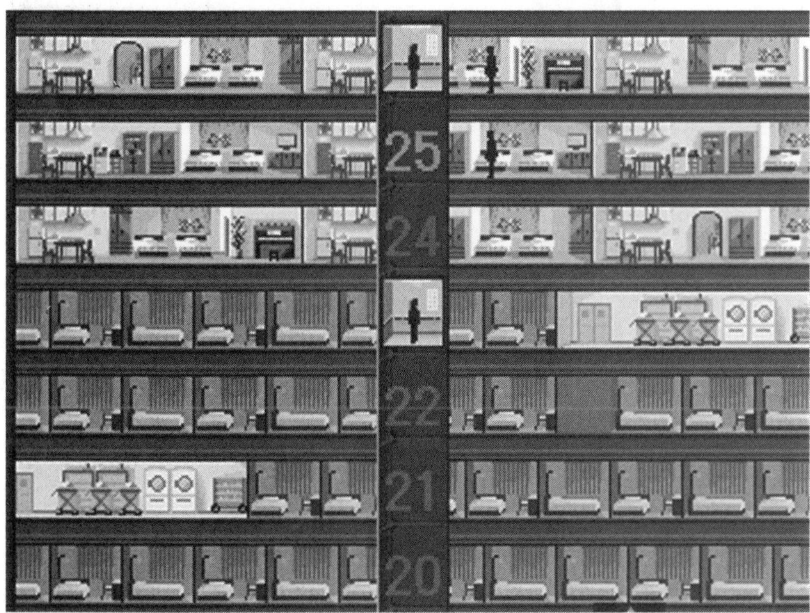

Figure 7-1. Residential Area. Live-in tenants and overnight visitors help keep your tower in balance—both aesthetically and financially.

Hotel rooms, for example, bring in regular daily returns—small, sometimes, but regular. On the other hand, a Condo brings in a large, one-time-only influx of cash. Occupants of both types of dwellings become regular customers for commercial zones, regardless of weather. This adds to the stability of a tower's economy. A substantial residential community helps reduce your building's reliance on sunny days for economic health.

Of course, residential tenants do tend to be more picky about services and conditions. Noise, in particular, irritates them. They do not tolerate nearby commercial neighbors for long, nor do they put up with ill-conceived transportation systems.

Condos

I like to think of *SimTower's* condominium units as "instant loans." Your *SimTower* User's Manual describes them similarly, suggesting that Condos are "somewhat like banks"—you build one, then sell it for about twice what you paid. Do you see why all those slick guys in suits get into real estate development?

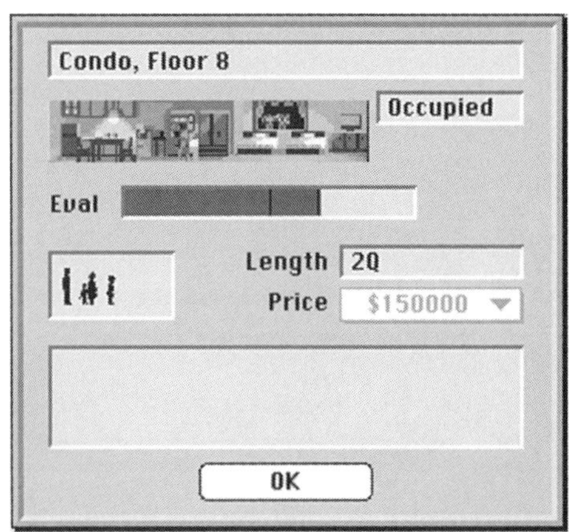

Figure 7-2. Condo People. The guy in the yellow boxers is your typical Condo head-of-household. His purchase of this dwelling provides a nice, big infusion of cash for your development schemes.

Condo development does have its drawbacks, however. Once built and sold, condos generate no additional income, nor do they produce any significant traffic for your tower's commercial areas. Despite their size, Condos hold only three inhabitants apiece (four, actually, if you count the Kid who's attached to the Woman).

Also, if you destroy a Condo or its dwellers run out of patience with your property management skills and move out, the original sales price is deducted from your cash balance.

So, you'd better build your Condo developments in well-serviced areas. Since you can't manipulate their sentiments with rent reductions, you have to keep their elevators running smoothly.

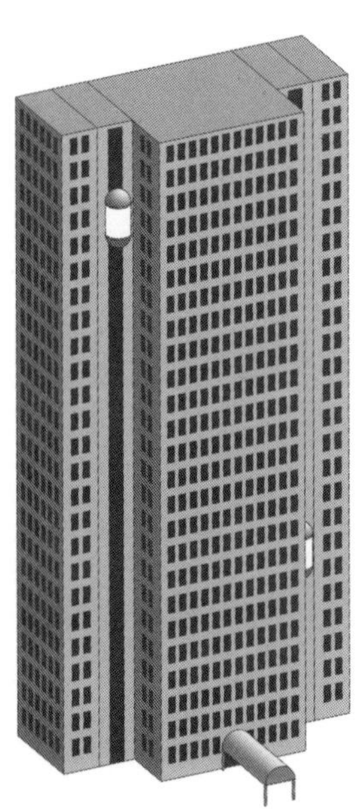

Condo Pricing

Condos cost $80,000 to build and can be sold at four price points, ranging from $40,000 to $200,000. Obviously, it would be foolish to build something for $80,000 and sell it for half that—especially since Condos sales are one-time-only, with no subsequent rent paid to you. But remember: The higher the Condo sales price, the more picky your Condo dwellers are about noise and transportation issues.

The default sale price of a Condo is $150,000. If you want to raise that to $200,000 or lower it to $100,000, you have to make the change quickly. Condos are popular. If built on floors connected by transportation, they sell quickly.

Here's the best way to change your Condo sales price:

1. After you click to place your Condo, immediately move the pointer to the pause button on the Tool Bar.
2. Keep your eye on those little construction guys building the Condo. The instant the For Sale sign goes up, click on the Tool Bar pause button.
3. Now select the Magnifying Glass and click on your Condo to open its Facility Window.
4. Click and hold on the Price Window to open the drop-down menu.
5. Drag the cursor to highlight your desired sales price, then release.
6. Click on the Tool Bar play button to continue.

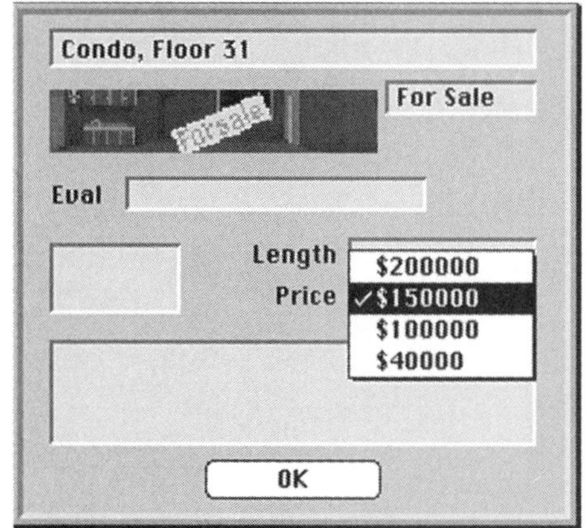

Figure 7-3. Condo Pricing. Here's the range of prices you can charge for your *SimTower* Condos.

Figure 7-4. Hot Items. Remember, Condos sell fast. This For Sale sign won't last long if you've got transportation connected.

One other minor sales note. Condos will sell on any day of the quarter, but they won't sell after 9:00 P.M. So, if you want the income from a Condo sale for that day, build before then. Otherwise, you'll have to wait until 7:00 A.M. the next morning to rack up the sale.

TIP Never sell a Condo at the $40,000 price point—unless you're an idiot, in which case you have my blessing.

Condo Dweller Habits

Condo dwellers consist of remarkably homogeneous family folks. In fact, they are so nuclear in their arrangement that I call them "nukes." Scan a few Condos with the Magnifying Glass during early morning or late evening hours. You'll find that every Condo

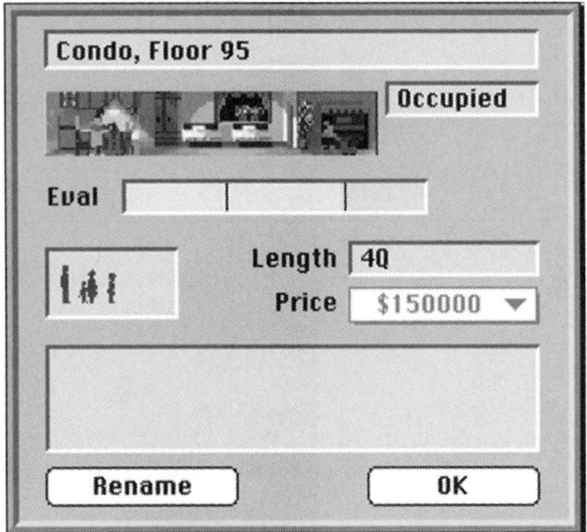

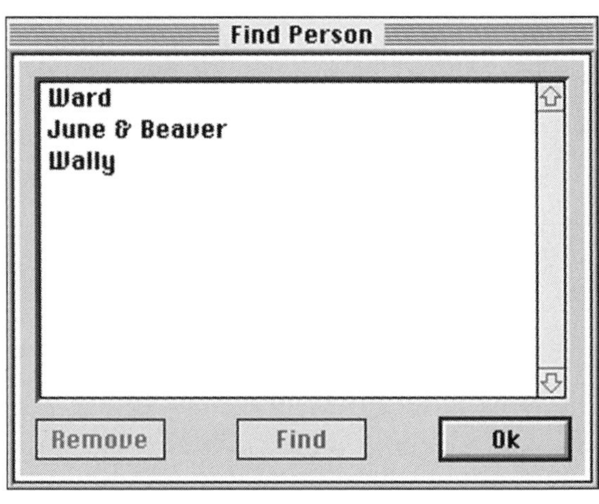

Figure 7-5.
Condo Dweller Habits.
I suspect not even the Cleavers could match the typical SimTower Condo-dwelling family for regularity and traditional Eisenhower-era values—though Wally arrives home a bit late sometimes, and Ward tends to wander around without his pants on.

houses one man, one "woman with kid," and one child. Pick out a family and name all the members. Then follow their day's routine. It makes Ozzie & Harriet look like radical countercultural activity.

The Condo man—let's call him Ward—leaves the tower for work each morning and dutifully returns each evening. The Condo child—let's call him Wally—leaves the tower for school each morning, and he, too, dutifully returns each evening. The Condo "woman with kid"—let's call them June and Beaver—stay home until noon, then traipse off to lunch in the lobby or out for shopping sprees in Men's Clothing or elsewhere. When June's not shopping, she's tidying up the castle—vacuuming obsessively, dusting, picking stuff off the floor.

Occasionally, you'll see permissive variations on this routine. Sometimes June and Beaver hit the sack alone at 9:00 P.M.—lights out. Then Ward staggers home about 10:00 P.M.—lights go on, he dresses, lights go out again. Finally, little Wally sneaks in about 11:00 P.M. . . . or later. Even though it's a weekday. Hey, what's his excuse? I want to know, man. (Apparently, those school bus commuter lines are hell.)

On weekends, condo folks get frisky. On Sunday, 25 percent of them eat lunch at the fast food places, 25 percent eat dinner in the restaurants, and 50 percent stay at home.

Condo Noise Problems

Condo owners are good neighbors . . . to each other, anyway. But they're quite snooty about non-Condo neighbors—except, of course, for Security or Medical units. (Condo owners love security.) The noise, in particular, just about sends them through the roof.

If you absolutely must put offices, shops, dining, cinema, or hotel rooms on the same floor with a Condo, you need to leave at least 31 sections of open floor space between them and the Condo. Otherwise, your Condo tenants whine and complain, then vacate after a few quarters, forcing you to buy back the Condo at the original sales price.

Of course, 31 sections is a lot of empty floor. (For an illustration of just how ridiculously wasteful this is, check out Figure 7-6.) Really, it's much more efficient to simply build all-Condo floors.

Figure 7-6. Here, you can see how much space is wasted when you leave the required noise buffer (at least 31 open floor sections) between a Condo and its non-Condo neighbor.

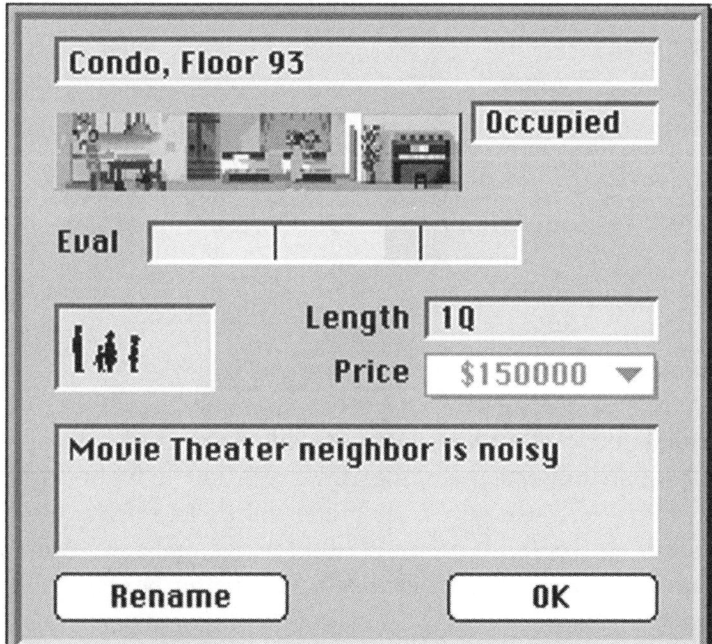

Figure 7-7. Uh-oh. You've got noisy neighbors too close to your Condo dwellers.

Build Condo-only floors. This eliminates noise problems and lets you avoid wasteful buffers of open floor.

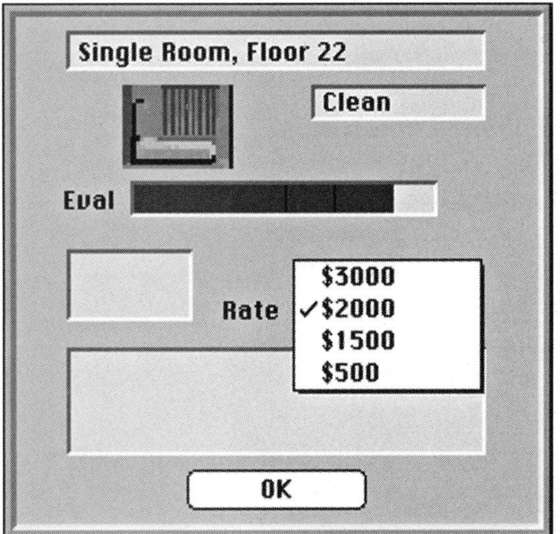

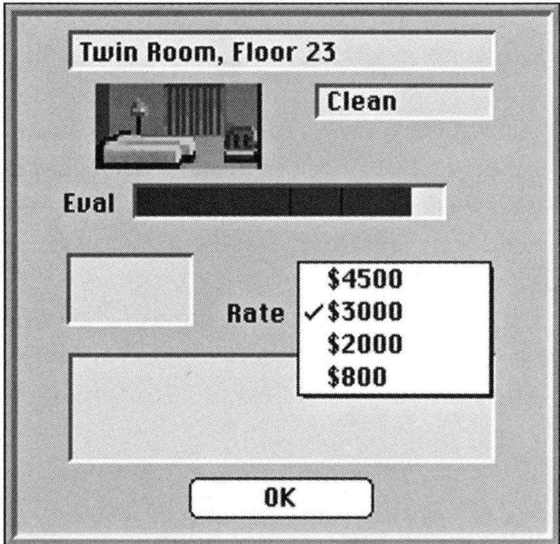

Figure 7-8. Shall I Put That On Your Credit Cards, Sir? Here are your three hotel room choices with their Rate Windows open. Is it me, or does $9,000 a night seem a little steep?

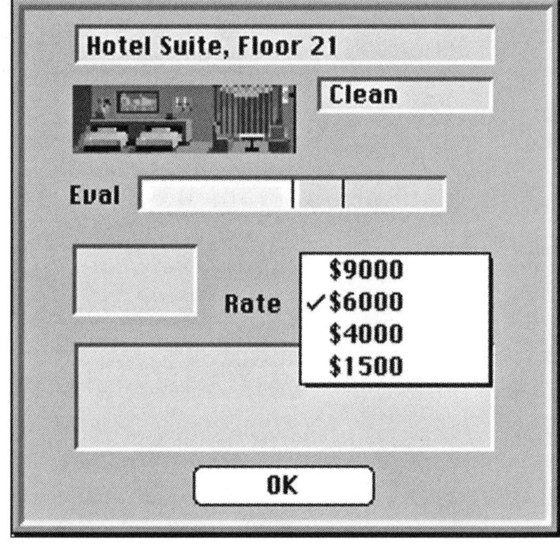

Hotels

Hotels provide a nice source of daily cash. And I do mean cash. Can you imagine plunking down $3,000 a night for a Single Room? For those prices, the Hotel shuttle had better be a Harrier Jump-Jet. And who drops $9,000 for one night in a Suite? Forget the wrapped chocolates, man—there'd better be something *special* on my pillow. Diamonds. A spotted owl. I want rare value for my money. Bow to me when I pass. That kind of thing.

What does any of this have to do with *SimTower* strategy? The answer: Nothing whatsoever. So, let's get back to the original point. Hotels provide regular daily income. As you expand your

Hotel floors, this amount can become significant—or at least enough to provide fun money while you wait for your big quarterly score of rental cash from Offices and Shops.

Hotel Routine

Visitors start checking in at 5:00 P.M. As each room is rented, it lights up and the shades draw open. Then guests arrive and unpack. After settling in, 50 percent of the hotel visitors head out to dine. This complicates the transportation scenario a bit. With people arriving and departing from the same floors at the same time, elevator scheduling needs to be very flexible.

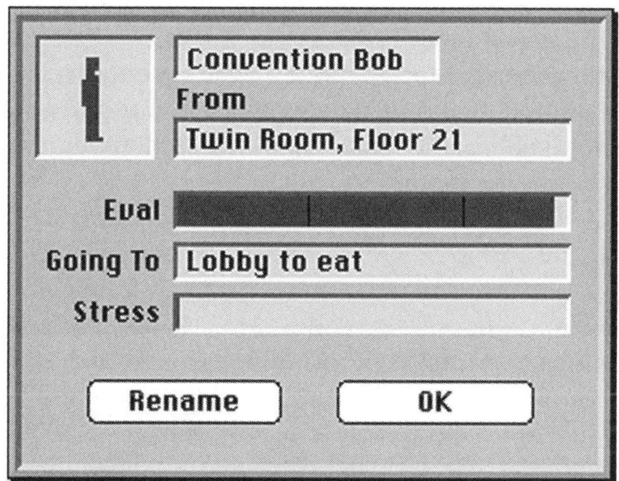

Figure 7-9. Hotel Diner. Bob, in town for a convention, heads out in search of fine dining. Remember that 50 percent of your other hotel visitors will do likewise.

The next morning, guests begin to check out at 6:30 A.M. and continue to exit throughout the morning, until 12:00 noon. As guests leave, your crack corps of housekeepers leaps into action. This routine never changes. It remains the same for all three days of the quarter.

Housekeeping

Five-star hotel management may seem glamorous and sophisticated. But beneath its glitzy surface lurks an ever-present fear of dark, evil things—like dirt, bug infestation, wrinkled sheets, odd curtain stains. The kind of things all the cute little soaps in the world can't erase from a weary traveler's memory. In fact, only one thing staves off daily hostelry disaster. That's right—it's your Housekeeping staff.

Figure 7-10. Housekeeping. You can't have a hotel without a Housekeeping staff. Each unit is home to six highly trained maintenance personnel.

Each Housekeeping facility serves as base of operations for six maintenance experts. Housekeepers use stairs, but it's best to connect all hotel floors with a Service elevator. As guests leave in the morning, your cleaning staff works floor by floor, left to right, cleaning up rooms.

Remember that housekeepers work until only 5:00 P.M., when the new crop of guests arrives. Rooms they can't reach in time remain dirty and unoccupied, costing you a night's rent. But that's not all. If housekeepers can't reach a room three days in a row, it suddenly becomes a breeding ground for nasty, ineradicable legions of bugs. So, if you have dirty rooms at the end of the day, you'd better beef up your Housekeeping staff.

Once roaches invade a room, it can no longer be "cleaned." Worse, the infestation spreads to other Hotel rooms on that floor.

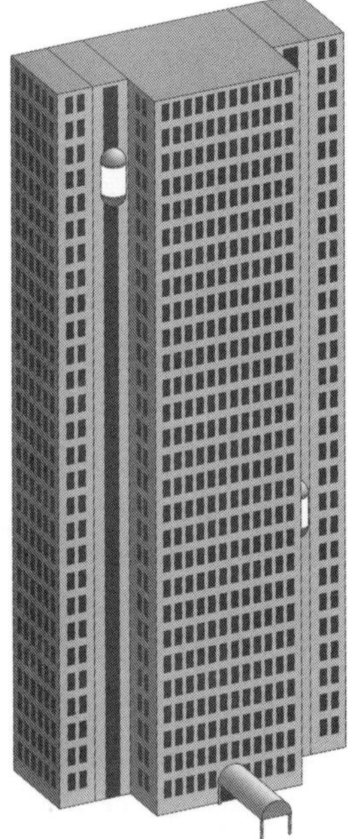

Figure 7-11. Morning Rush.
Here's a typical hotel check-out scene. Note where clean and dirty rooms are located. Housekeepers work each floor from left to right.

The only way to get rid of bugs is to bulldoze the infested rooms right away and start over. For more on this, see Hotel Bugs in Chapter 14: Special Events and Features.

TIP Immediately destroy any bug-infested Hotel room!

Figure 7-12. Bugs!
If you don't get your Housekeeping staff in gear, you'll have a bug infestation on your hands. Bugs spread quickly from room to room on a floor.

Hotel Noise Problems

Hotel visitors are sensitive to noise, though they're not quite as touchy as Condo dwellers. In fact, they don't mind being right next door to Condo folks—though, of course, the Condo will complain. Hotel guests can also roost peacefully next to Housekeeping, Medical, or Security facilities.

However, if you put any other type of tenant—shops, offices, fast food, or other entertainment—on the same floor, Hotel visitors complain unless at least 21 sections of empty floor space exist between their room and the noisy tenant.

TIP To minimize noise problems for your Hotel visitors, build Hotel-only floors.

PET
74
73
72
69

8 Commercial Zones

Well-planned commercial zones provide a significant chunk of your income. By "commercial" property, I'm referring to any kind of retail-oriented store or similar unit—retail shops (including banks and post offices), fast food joints, restaurants, and movie theaters. Think of a mall. In fact, think of many malls. A 100-story tower is big enough to support many layers of shopping.

Figure 8-1. Commercial-Zoned Area. A bustling commercial area keeps things lively in your tower (and your bank book).

Of course, any mall-like space must be carefully designed to pull in traffic and funnel it to tenants. Your *SimTower* commercial zones must also balance this need with the overall flow of the tower.

One other note: *SimTower* includes the Party Hall tool icon in the same drop-down menu as your other commercial tool icons. While a Party Hall isn't exactly a retail concern, it does share certain qualities and restrictions with other commercial entities, so we'll include it in our discussion of commercial zoning.

General Strategy

Always cluster retail shops, fast food, restaurants, and movie theaters within five floors of Sky Lobbies. Then connect these commercial floors to the Sky Lobby with escalators. After you've done that, you can eliminate Standard elevator service to those floors—i.e., click the Finger tool on the elevator-shaft numbers of your commercial-only floors.

Figure 8-2. A Fool Too Far. It's tough enough to be an entrepreneur without this kind of problem. Don't put commercial shops more than five floors from the Sky Lobby.

As a result, your elevators dump everyone at the Sky Lobby—rather than stopping at each commercial floor—and let shoppers and diners ride escalators up or down to their destinations. As you can imagine, this significantly cuts down passenger waiting time—you've eliminated five to ten stops!—and thus eliminates a lot of red-faced stress.

(For a more detailed, floor-by-floor look at this strategy of creating elevator/escalator synergy in commercial zones, see Figure 12-2 in Chapter 12.)

If you layer your tower vertically in this manner, you'll find that each 15-floor increment seems to possess a life of its own. From 12:00-1:00 P.M. on business workdays, your Fast Food shops will be packed with Office workers. These workers almost always hail from Offices within 8-10 floors above the place where they are dining. (Interestingly, when Sims seek eating destinations, they always travel down to the next Sky Lobby area, rather than up.)

Always develop commercial areas within five floors above or below your Sky Lobbies.

Figure 8-3. Finger Your Commercial Floors.
After connecting your shopping floors to the Sky Lobby with escalators, cancel elevator service to those floors.

Fast Food

Sims are busy folks. They often eat on the run, and so they appreciate dining convenience. Fast food outlets, then, are a natural for your tower. When kept within easy reach of busy Sky Lobbies, a burger joint can be a popular and quite profitable enterprise.

When you build a Fast Food shop, *SimTower* randomly places one of five different kinds of eateries in the space you select—Chinese Cafe, Coffee Shop, Japanese Soba, Ice Cream, or Hamburger Stand. (See Figure 8-4.) Of course, you are free to individualize each one with a clever, appetizing name.

SimTower Fast Food joints open daily at 10 A.M. They do the bulk of their business at lunchtime (12:00-1:00 P.M.), though diners continue to trickle in to well-placed shops throughout the afternoon and evening. The Income (or Loss) from these operations is added to (or subtracted from) your cash balance daily at 9:00 P.M., when all Fast Food outlets close.

SimTower Fast Food Operations (Daily)

Patronage	Evaluation	Comment	Profit (Loss)
10-24	Red	"Very Few Customers"	($3,000)
25-34	Yellow	"Business is Average"	$2,000
35-49	Blue	"Business is Good"	$3,000
50-Above	Blue	"Business is Very Good!"	$5,000

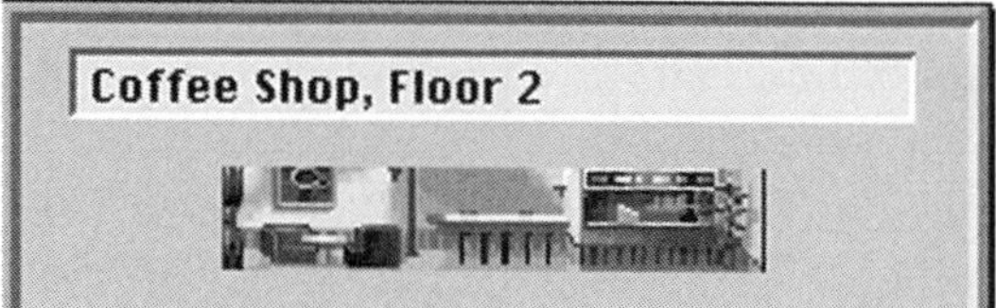

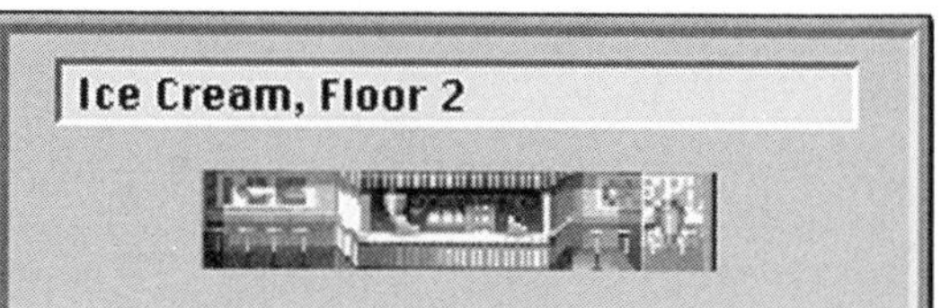

Figure 8-4.
Here are the five types of Fast Food shops available for placement in your tower.

Where to Place Fast Food Operations

Build Fast Food outlets anywhere in your commercial zones within five floors of a Sky Lobby. If your elevator system is sound and escalators run from the Sky Lobby to all floors of the commercial zone, your Fast Food traffic should grow steadily. You should get plenty of lunch business from nearby Offices, especially those in the same "zone" (that is, bounded by the same Sky Lobbies above and below).

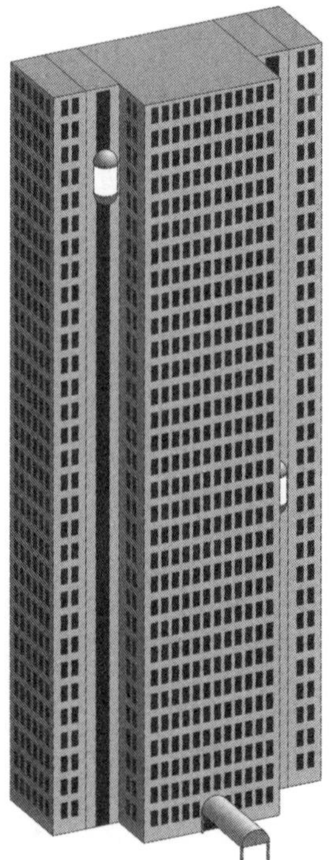

Figure 8-5.
Rainy Days and Sundays. The first three keys to Fast Food success are location, location, and location. But weather and weekend shopping habits can affect customer traffic, as well.

Also remember that *SimTower* movie theater audiences are ravenous, and often want to eat both before and after movies are shown. Again, if your Fast Food shops are well connected (via escalator) to your movie theaters, you can reap the benefits of cinema crowd hunger.

Restaurants

SimTower's finer dining establishments open daily at 5:00 P.M. and close at 11:00 P.M. Frankly, at $200,000 apiece, they seem a rather pricey investment. Even when running at full capacity, Restaurants dump only $6,000 of income per day into your cash balance. At that rate, they don't pay back their building costs for at least 11 *SimTower* quarters—and that doesn't take into account the usual early operating losses, nor the inevitable bad days due to rain and other factors.

So why build restaurants? Good question. They look cool. OK, so there's that. Let's see. They stay open late? They class up the joint? Is any of this working for you?

Actually, any investment that eventually pays itself off and turns into pure income is worthwhile, depending on the patience of the investor. But let's look at a comparable investment. Suppose that instead of building a Restaurant, you took the same money and built two Retail Shops. You charge the default average rent for shops—$15,000 per quarter apiece. At that rate, the two shops repay the original investment of $200,000 in seven quarters—more than a year sooner than the break-even point for a Restaurant. And as traffic builds, you can raise both Retail Shop rents to the premium level of $20,000.

Figure 8-6.
Here are the four types of Restaurants available for placement in your tower.

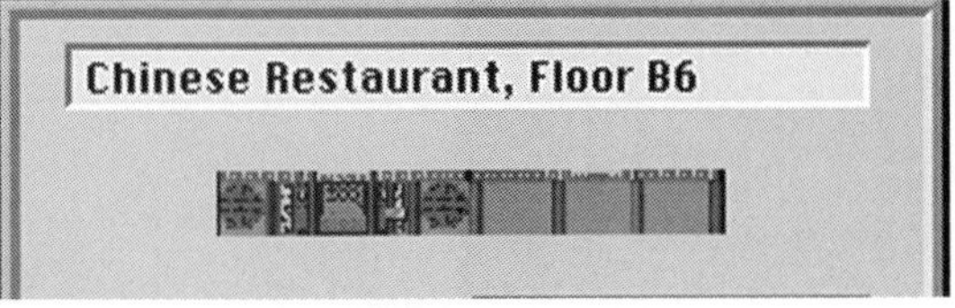

Sushi Bar, Floor B7

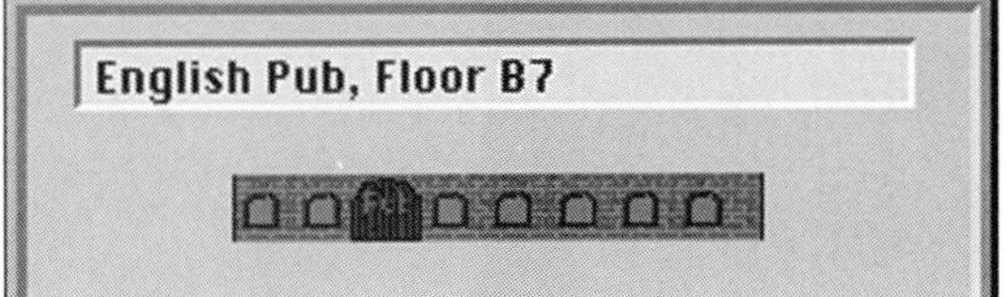

Now, that represents a long-term income of $40,000 per quarter for two Retail Shops, versus $18,000 per quarter for a Restaurant—both for the same original investment of $200,000. Think about it. Is the luxury of fine dining in your tower worth that? Your decision.

SimTower Restaurant Operations (Daily)

Patronage	Evaluation	Comment	Profit (Loss)
10-24	Red	"Very Few Customers"	($6,000)
25-34	Yellow	"Business is Average"	$4,000
35 (max)	Blue	"Business is Good"	$6,000

NOTE Restaurants cannot accommodate more than 35 diners per night.

Where to Place Restaurants

Restaurants belong anywhere in your commercial zones—that is, within five floors of a Sky Lobby. All of your patrons come from outside the tower, but the patronage grows if there is a Movie Theater nearby. Of course, Restaurants are closed during the first movie (shown from 1:00-4:00 P.M.), but they can catch some of the cinema run-off after the second show lets out at 8:00 P.M. Again, this only works if your Restaurants are well connected via escalator to your Movie Theaters.

NOTE Poor traffic or rainy days can result in operating losses, which are then subtracted from your Cash Balance at 11:00 P.M.

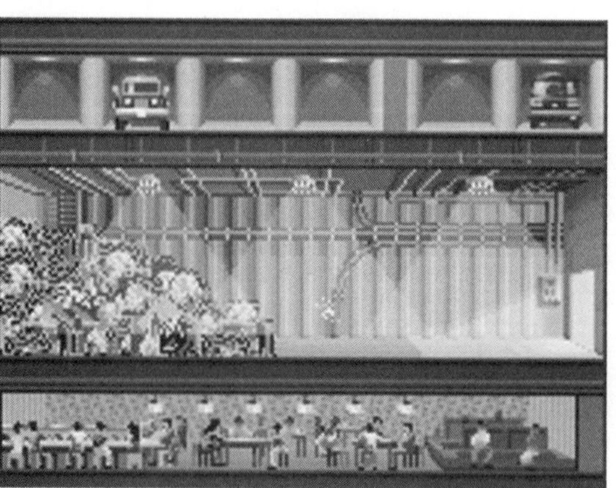

Figure 8-7. Ignorance Is Bliss. Hmmm. These underground sushi lovers don't seem to mind that they're dining under parked cars . . . and just a few feet away from huge mounds of garbage.

Retail Shops

Dollar for dollar, Retail Shops are probably the best investment you can make in your tower. In terms of both rental income and tower population, shops provide excellent growth numbers. In fact, I suggest that the bulk of your commercial zones be filled with retail concerns—Pet Stores, Flower Shops, Banks, Boutiques, Book Stores, and all the other tenants that keep towers lively and profitable.

Figure 8-8.
Here are the 11 types of Retail Shops and related services available for placement in your tower.

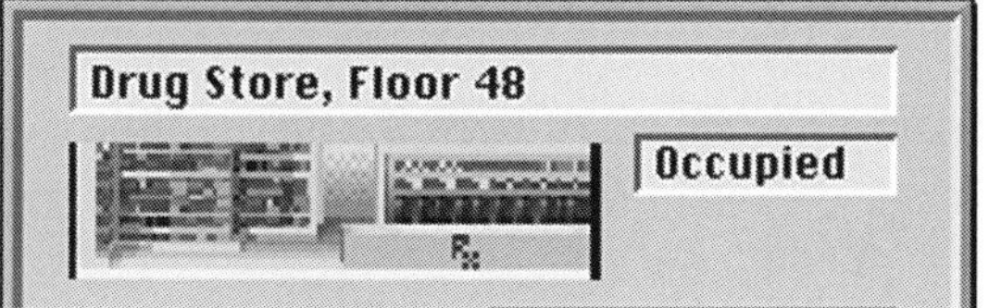

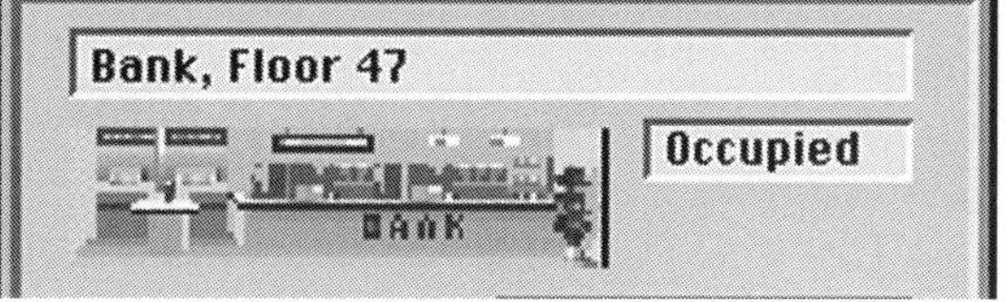

Retail Shops open daily at 10:00 A.M. Their rents are added to your cash balance on the first work day of each quarter at 5:00 A.M.

Remember that poorly planned transportation routes or rainy days can result in reduced traffic. If the number of customers drops, so does the store's evaluation level. Tenants stuck with terrible (red) evaluations for more than a quarter may go out of business and vacate the premises. If so, don't expect a new tenant to jump into the space right away. Chances are you'll have to lower the rent a bit; otherwise, it may take quite awhile to lure in new tenants.

(For more specific information on pricing and evaluation of shops and other facilities, see Chapter 13.)

Figure 8-9. Ah, Shoppers. If you put your nose close enough to the screen, you can smell the money.

Where to Place Retail Shops

Retail Shops can flourish anywhere in a standard commercial zone (that is, developed within five floors of a Sky Lobby). Most of your shop customers come from outside the tower, but a few Condo dwellers browse through your stores, as well. Shop patronage grows if there is a Movie Theater within five floors and if it is well connected by escalators.

Always put Shops within five floors of both lobbies and movie theaters.

Figure 8-10. Shopping Area. Here's a successful scheme for a shopping area. Cluster stores around a movie theater, then connect all floors with escalators.

Cinema

Movie theaters are a terrific draw, pulling traffic into shops and food places. A sellout at the box office can bring 40 to 50 people into a commercial area—people who will dine before or after films, browse through retail stores, use post offices or banking services or whatever else is available in your commercial center.

Each movie theater shows its film twice daily, once from 1:00-4:00 P.M., then again from 5:00-8:00 P.M. Box office receipts are added to your cash balance daily when the theaters close at 8:00 P.M. And as at real movie theaters, you'll have to change your movies regularly. In *SimTower*, your movies continue to show successfully for one year. After that, you can choose a replacement—if you've got the cash.

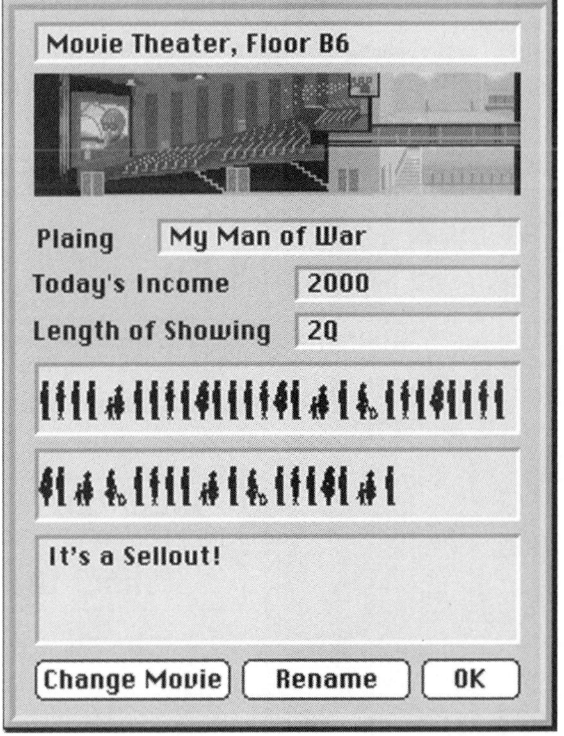

Figure 8-11. It's a Sellout! And so are you! But it's great, isn't it?

First-run films are classified as "latest movies" and cost a cool $300,000. You can also select a "classic" for $150,000. On classics, you'll get steady sales for a year, but no sellouts at the box office.

Figure 8-12. Terrible Sales! Time to change the feature presentation. Unfortunately, it's not cheap. But it's worth it.

Figure 8-13.Change Movies. What can you afford?

SimTower Cinema Box Office				
	1Q	2Q	3Q	4Q / Over One Year
Latest Films	Sellout!	Sellout!	Average	Terrible! Change the movie!
Classic Films	Average	Average	Average	Terrible! Change the movie!

For fun, here's a look at the movies, latest and classic, that play in your theaters. Have you seen them all yet? By the way, these shots, taken from the Macintosh 1.1 version of *SimTower*, each contain an on-screen typo which the Macintosh 1.2 version doesn't have. Challenge yourself to find it! Challenge your friends! Challenge Dan Quayle!

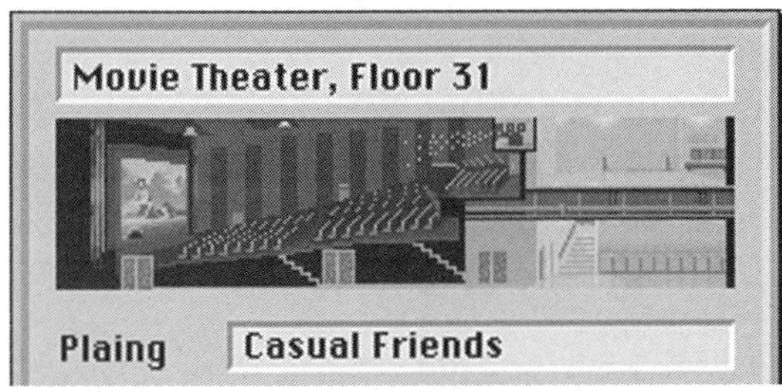

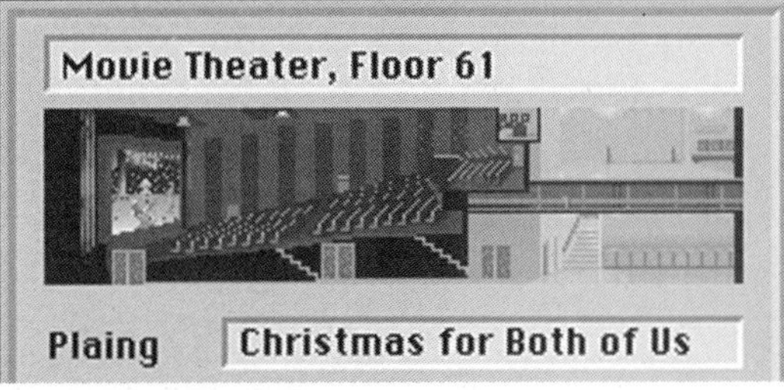

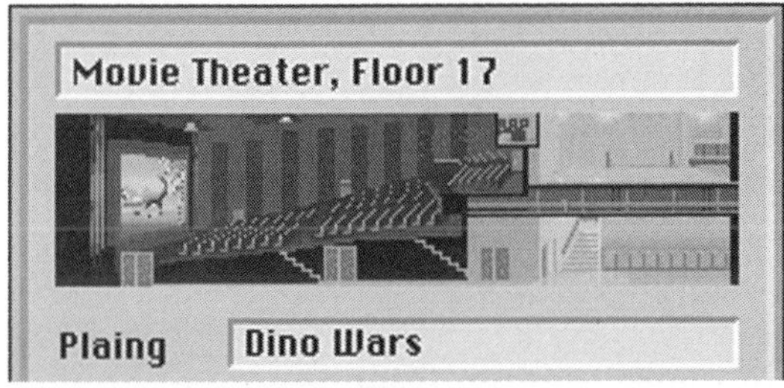

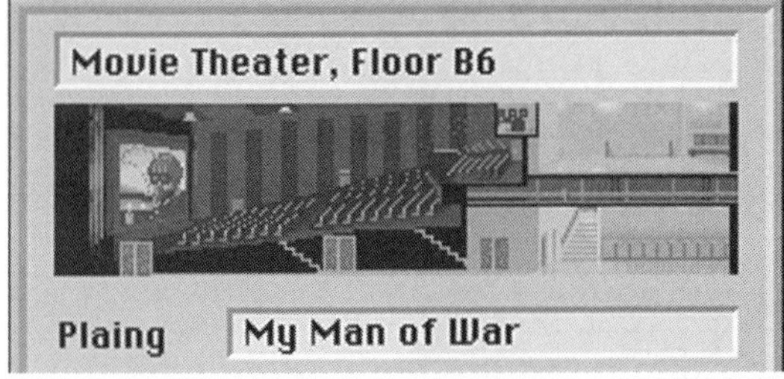

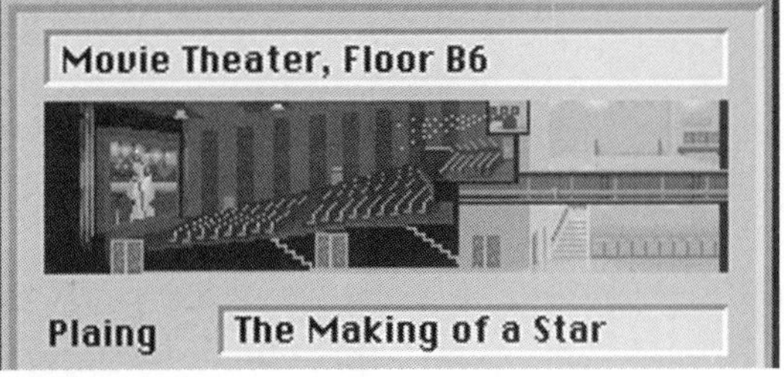

Figure 8-14.
First-Run ("Latest") Films.

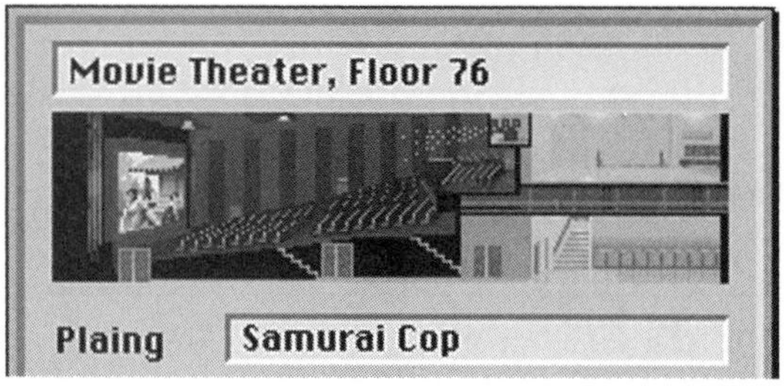

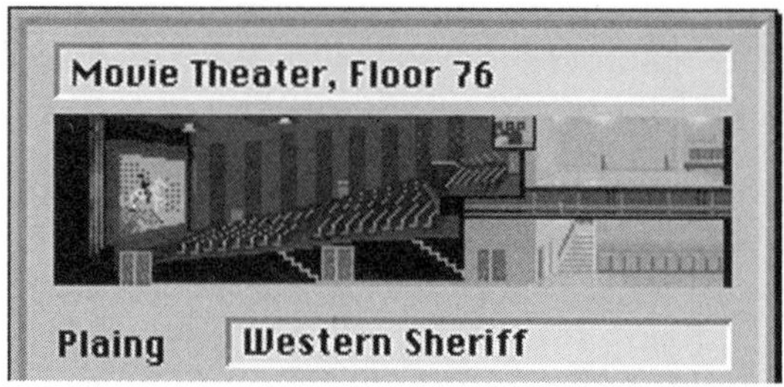

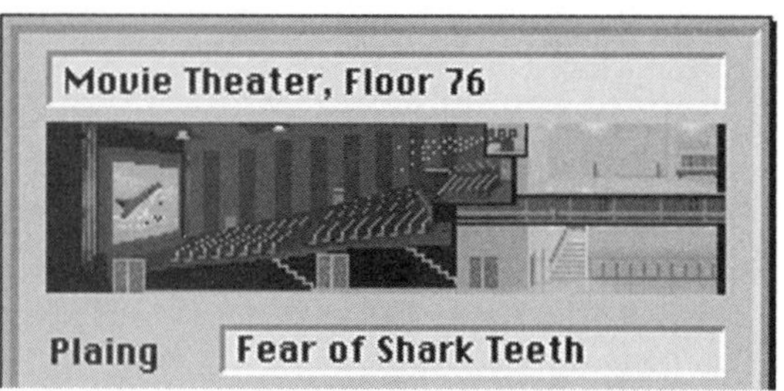

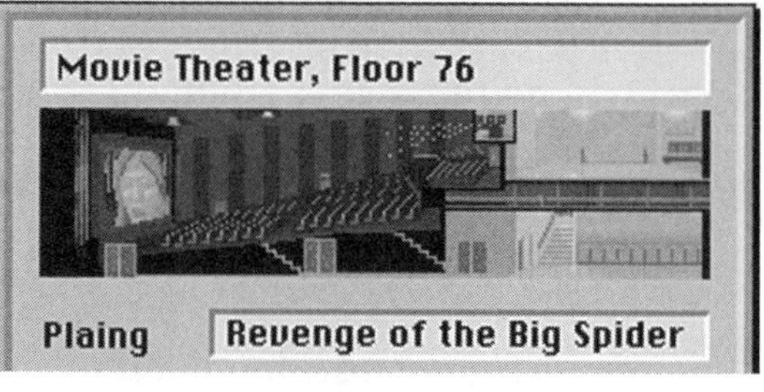

Figure 8-15. Classic Films.

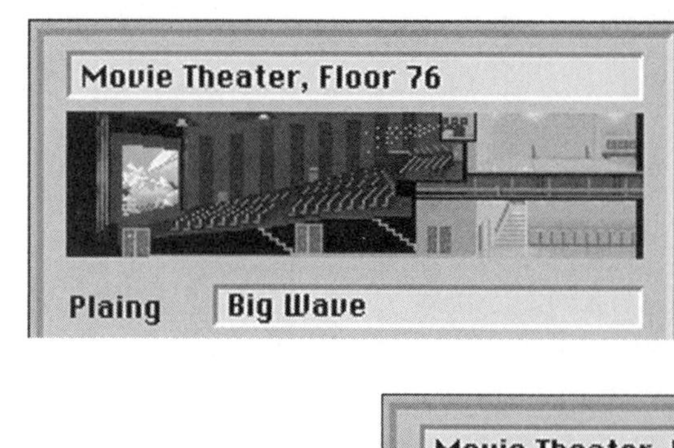

Movie Theater, Floor 76

Where to Place Movie Theaters

Movie theaters increase your commercial traffic for five floors in either direction, up and down. Thus, the best place to build your two-level theaters is on the two floors directly above or below a Sky Lobby.

Figure 8-16.
Cinema Placement.
Here's the best place to put your movie theater—in the two floors just above or below a Sky Lobby (in this case, the Floor 60 Sky Lobby).

Party Halls

Your local mall has a lot of things, but it probably doesn't have a Party Hall. Indeed, one usually associates Party Halls with a hotel, rather than a mall. Yet the Party Halls in *SimTower* belong in your commercial zone, not in your hotel (or anyplace else). Noise from a Party Hall annoys any office or residential tenant, including hotel guests.

Actually, *SimTower* Party Halls don't have to be within five floors of a Sky Lobby to gain maximum occupancy. In fact, you can build a profitable Party Hall in any area connected by transportation to the ground-floor lobby. But again, Party Halls are too noisy for Condo, Hotel, or Office neighbors, unless you want to leave the appropriate noise buffer of open floor on either side. Since Party Halls are also two-level structures, these noise buffers would create a lot of open, wasted space on two separate floors.

Figure 8-17. Party Time! Looks like fun, though I get nervous under big chandeliers. I hope they keep those kids away from the punch bowl.

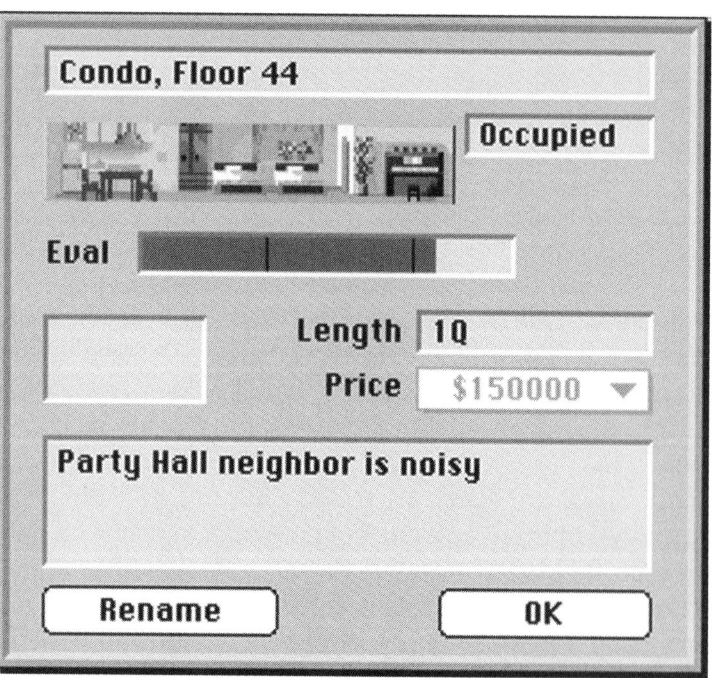

Figure 8-18. It's Too Noisy? Next to a Party Hall? Geez, I thought I was the center of the universe, and everybody else was supposed to whisper.

So, again, it's best to build Party Halls in commercial areas. Although the user's manual indicates that you require a specified number of Hotel rooms for Party Halls to flourish, you'll note that all of your party guests come from "Outside."

Party Hall Routine

Lights go on at 1:00 P.M., and people start to trickle in after that. Once you get your full compliment of 50 guests, things are in full swing. At 5:00 P.M., the party's over, my friend, and its time to open the cash drawer. A busy hall will bring in a hefty $20,000 per day.

PET
PET
74
73
72
69

9 Tower Facilities

A tower is a complex, powerful organism. It must be maintained and nurtured. It must be protected. After all, your Sim tenants expect a lot for the daily or quarterly money they shovel into your pockets. So part of your job as landlord is to provide some basic tower services and facilities.

Security

Once your tower has been promoted to a two-star rating by that little team of virtual judges inserted by *SimTower* into your computer, you will be rewarded with the addition of a Security tool in the Tool Bar. Now, with your new Sim power tool, you can place up to 10 rooms full of goons . . . er, security experts . . . throughout your edifice.

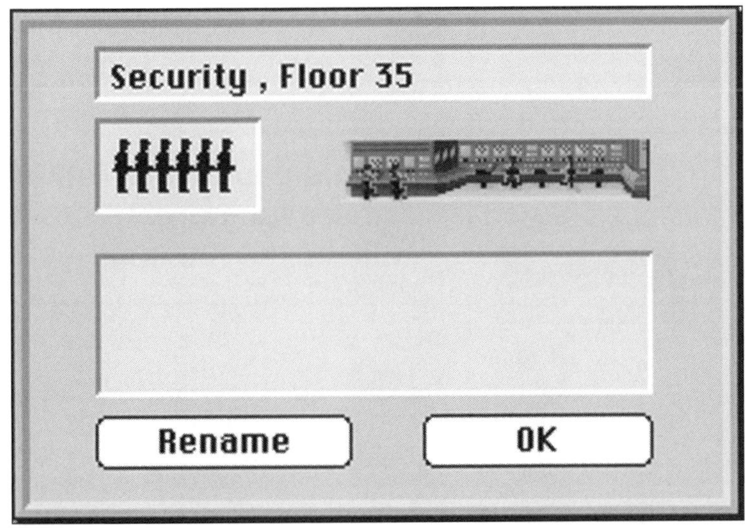

Figure 9-1. Security. There's nothing like it. Without it, you're a cowering, quivering, vulnerable landlord.

As you can see in Figure 9-1, each Security unit consists of six rugged neo-cops sitting around a high-tech control center, drinking coffee and making jokes about liberals. Most of the time, this is the extent of their job. But every once in a while, a true emergency arises—like a fire or a bomb threat. Then, if you choose to deploy them . . . it's SWAT time!

Of course, you can pay off the terrorists or bring in an emergency helicopter fire crew. Sure, go ahead—just throw money at the problem. (Why don't you run for Congress while you're at it?) But isn't it so much more satisfying to hunt down the threat with relentless platoons of rabidly loyal tower militiamen, the kind of guys who would fall on a grenade to protect the lobby art?

You bet it is.

How Much Security Is Necessary?

Blackmail from Terrorists!
They demand $300000 or a hidden bomb will explode at 3 O'clock.
Pay Them
Find the Bomb

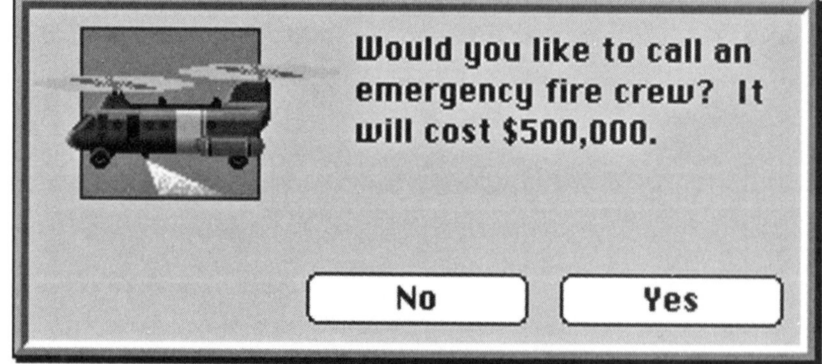
Would you like to call an emergency fire crew? It will cost $500,000.
No
Yes

Figure 9-2. Disasters Aren't Cheap. But with lots of well-placed Security cops, you won't have to fork over these kinds of ransoms.

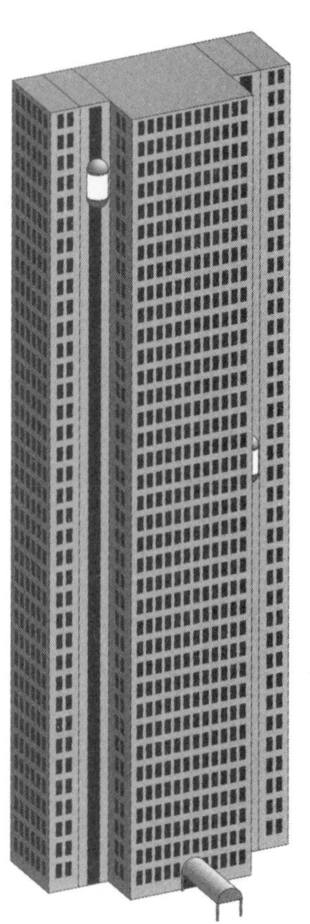

Each Security unit costs $100,000. Believe me, that's cheap. Compared with the cumulative cost of paying off terrorists or hiring fire crews—or even worse, the cost of repairing bomb or fire damage to your tower—well, the $1 million tab for placing all 10 Security units amounts to chump change.

Don't believe me? Just add it up. Bombers return every five years after the first extortion attempt. Fire comes back to haunt you every seven years. Payoffs cost you $300,000 per bomb, $500,000 per fire crew. So after only one cycle of one disaster apiece, you've already paid out $800,000. Two cycles, and the million you could have paid for Security seems like the deal of the century.

That's assuming you have the money for the payouts in the first place. If a terrorist strikes a Security-free tower and you don't have the ransom payoff, all you can do is wait for the Big Boom—then watch a huge, multimillion-dollar chunk of your tower blasted into charcoal briquettes.

Figure 9-3. You're Getting Hotter . . . Hotter. But you won't find much relief if you don't have enough Security guys to keep pace with a fire's inexorable march.

Fire can be even worse. Fires can't ignite until you reach a three-star rating, and you can't receive a three-star rating unless you've placed at least two Security units in your tower. But if you stop there (with only two Security units) and add no more Security, a fire can literally lay waste to your entire building. If the fire starts far away from Security facilities, your tiny contingent of 12 troopers may not have a snowball's chance in hell (an apt metaphor) against the quick-spreading inferno.

Where to Place Security Facilities

Security forces spread out from their Security facility, one guy per floor. Three guards go up from their headquarters, and three go down. This "three-up/three-down" pattern is always the same. So don't overlap Security facilities by placing them within three floors of each other. You'll end up with two guys on the same floor, doing the job of one—a real waste of resources.

As for overall placement strategy, just do some simple math:

You are limited to 10 Security facilities per tower. Your tower has a height limit of 100 stories, plus 10 underground floors, for a total of 110 floors. Therefore, it's best to put one Security Center every 11 floors or so, including one underground.

TIP Build Security facilities approximately every 11 floors.

Medical Centers

The minute you achieve a three-star rating for your tower, your Sims begin to clamor for medical facilities. You should always place Medical Centers near lobbies, as your tenants demand—preferably just one floor above or below a lobby.

1st WD/4Q/1st Year
Offices or Condos demand Medical Center near Lobby
Fund $197000
Pop 1109

Figure 9-4. Is There a Doctor in the House? If not, you'd better build a Medical Center soon. And you'd better put it where they want it, near the lobby.

Keep in mind that Medical Centers are *big* suckers—26 floor sections wide, in fact. At $500,000 apiece, they're expensive, too. Don't worry if you're a little short on cash, though. You can survive just fine without a hospital. You may lose a disgruntled worker or two, but most Sims don't need medical attention immediately, if at all. However, you'll never graduate to a four-star rating without a Medical Center.

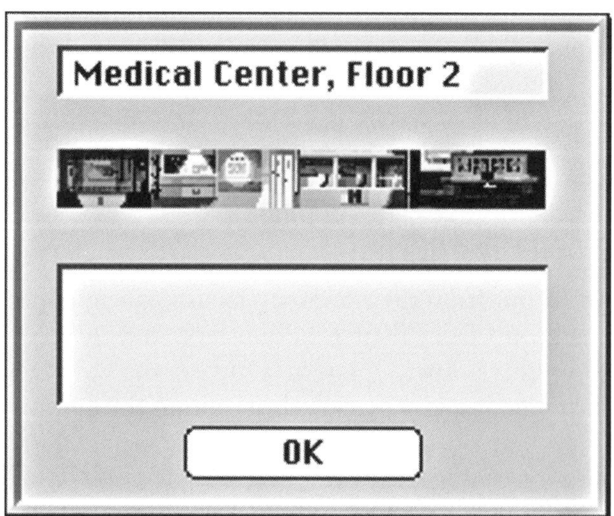

Figure 9-5. Medical Center. It's expensive, but no tower worth its stars is without one.

In some situations, you may have to plan ahead before placing a Medical Center. If you can't afford one just now but tenants are demanding one in a particular area, activate the Medical Center tool to measure out the space you'll need. Then build around that space, waiting to fill in the Medical Center until after you get your next big influx of quarterly income.

Parking

Wimpy little buildings can get by with surface street parking. But no tower of substance can flourish without a significant parking structure of its very own. Indeed, once your *SimTower* skyscraper reaches three-star status, your tenants vigorously demand parking facilities.

1st WD/4Q/1st Year
Office workers demand Parking
Fund $195000
Pop 1110

Figure 9-6. Parking Demand. Better give them what they want.

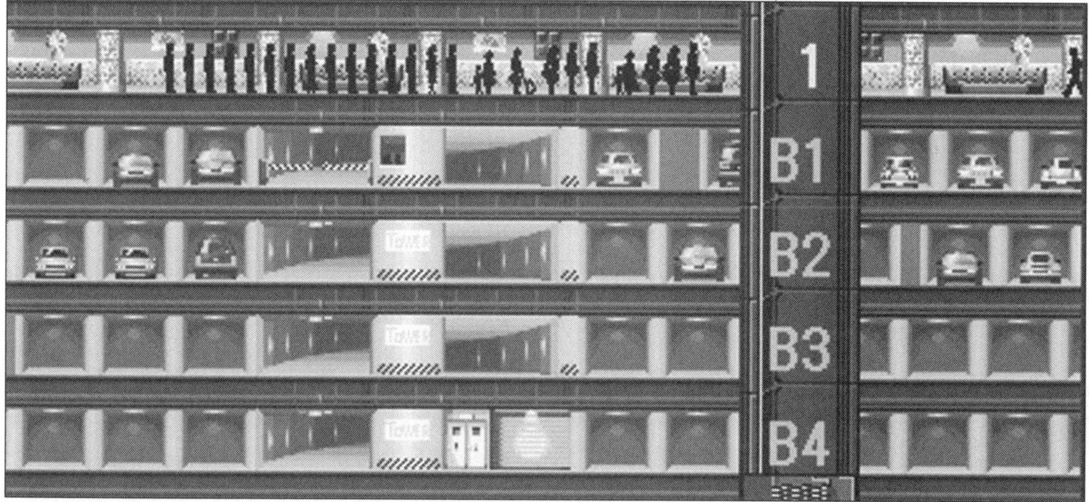

Figure 9-7. Acres of Parking. A good multi-star tower needs parking . . . lots of it.

Parking Ramps

Underground parking structures prove quite useless without ramps connecting them to the street. So, when you're ready to develop a tower parking zone, the very first step is to place a parking ramp on level B1. This first ramp is your automatic-gate entrance. Even if you don't have parking spaces on B1, you still have to build the automatic gate on that level.

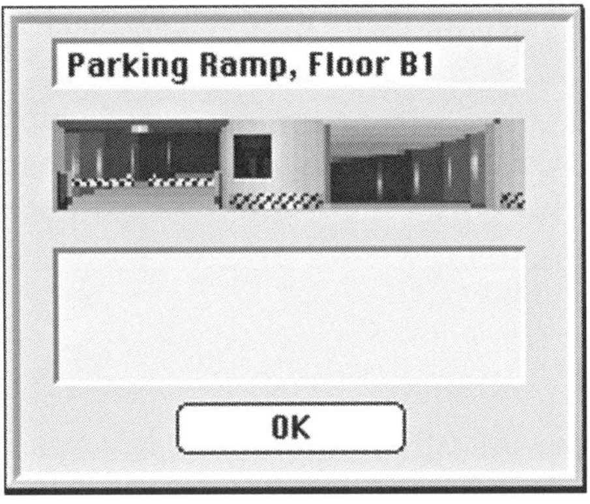

Figure 9-8. Parking Ramp. All the parking stalls in the world bring you zero benefit without a ramp structure to connect them to the street.

Figure 9-9. Stack O' Ramps. Parking ramps must be stacked vertically, with the first one—the automatic gate—constructed on level B1.

All of your parking ramps must be built in a vertical stack, as seen in Figure 9-9. Of course, this only makes structural sense.

Parking Stalls

With a ramp installed, you can build accessible parking stalls. Each parking stall must be connected to a ramp. By "connected," I mean that parking stalls must run contiguously in either direction from the parking ramp on that level. Any gap consisting of a full stall width (four floor sections) or more causes a break in the connection. As a result, any stall placed after the gap becomes inaccessible and will be marked with a red "X."

Figure 9-10. "X" Marks the Spot. Red X's like these indicate that your parking spots aren't properly connected to a parking ramp.

However, stalls don't need to be perfectly adjacent to one another in order to remain connected to the ramp. Gaps less than a full stall width—that is, gaps less than four floor sections wide—do not break the string of connection. See Figure 9-11 for an illustration of this rule.

How Much Parking is Necessary?

The greatest demand for parking comes from your Office tenants. Fortunately, Offices are willing to share parking space. For every four Offices, you need only one stall in your underground structure. You also need one stall for every Hotel Suite in your tower. Condo owners, strangely enough, don't need parking spots (which seems a little odd, since they live there).

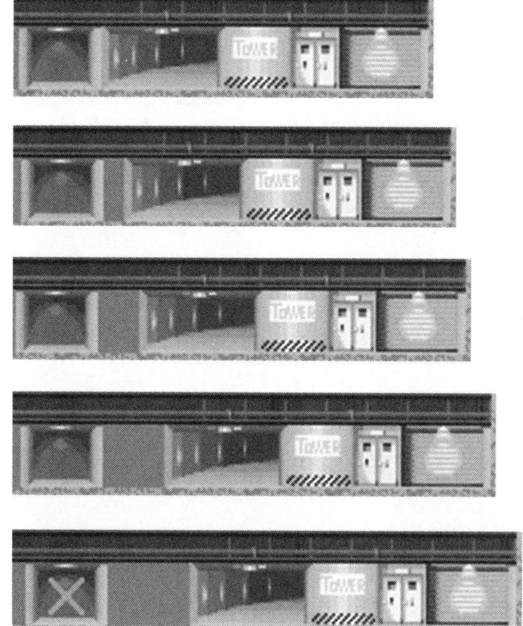

Figure 9-11. A Gap Too Far. As this series of shots illustrates, gaps of up to three floor sections wide do not break the connection between parking ramps and parking stalls. However, a four-section gap cuts the connection, as the "X" on the stall indicates.

Figure 9-12. Parking Stall. Build one for every four Offices in your tower, plus one for each Hotel Suite.

Recycling Centers

Once your tower reaches the three-star rating, it begins to generate some serious garbage. At that point, you'll get a message on the Info Bar telling you to build a Recycling Center. This is a large, two-level structure where trash is processed, then shipped out via garbage truck at 7:00 A.M. each day.

Recycling Centers must be built underground, and they cost a whopping $500,000 apiece. You'll need one Recycling Center for every 2,500 people who occupy your tower. You'll also need to connect a Service elevator to your Recycling Center.

Note that adjacent Recycling Centers can share a Service elevator. In other words, you can put Recycling Centers in any kind of configuration you want—horizontal row, vertical stack, L-shaped, whatever. Just make sure you keep them all interconnected by plac-

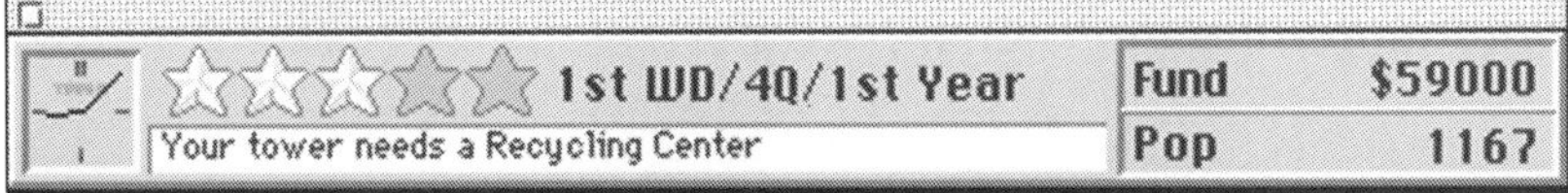

Figure 9-13. Time to Haul. Vertical empires are full of people who throw out stuff. Your job is to haul it away for them.

Figure 9-14. Garbage In, Garbage Out. Place new Recycling Centers adjacent (vertically or horizontally) to any existing Recycling Center. Ensure that a Service elevator runs down to at least one floor of one of the connected centers. In this illustration, it's floor B3 of the Recycling Center at the upper right.

ing each new Recycling Center adjacent (vertically or horizontally) to a previously placed center. Then you can run a single Service Elevator down to any one of your Recycling Centers.

The contents of the whole garbage complex gets hauled at 7:00 A.M. each morning (unless of course your bins are too full—in which case you must build additional Recycling Centers).

For more on how Service elevators work with Recycling Centers, see the Placing Service Elevators section in Chapter 12.

Metro Station

When you achieve a four-star rating, *SimTower* adds only one new construction tool to the Tool Bar. But it's a big, big addition. The tri-level Metro Station can be placed only on the bottom three underground floors of your tower—B8, B9, and B10. Once placed, the Metro's tunnel tube extends along floor B10 for the entire length of your working area.

You get only one Metro Station per tower, and it's a $1 million investment, so it might seem a bit frightening at first. But believe me, it's worth every penny. A Metro stop under your tower brings

Figure 9-15. Metro Station. The hub of the hubbub. With one of these in your tower, things will never be the same.

in great hordes of workers, shoppers, and diners. Be sure to have adequate elevator connections for passengers heading to above-ground destinations. As noted in the User's Manual, Metro passengers will work, live, or visit anywhere in your tower, as long as they have good transport up and down every day.

Figure 9-16. Metro Rush Hour. Your Metro Station swirls in a frenzy of activity sometimes . . .

Figure 9-17. . . . so be sure to have plenty of transportation connected, including both elevators and nearby escalators.

However, your User's Manual also notes that Metro passengers will shop and eat in stores and restaurants located on underground levels only. So it's probably wise to surround your Metro Station with a robust commercial zone and to connect its floors with escalators. This funnels Metro crowds directly into stores and takes some of the load off your elevators.

Here's one other note about Metro Station placement. In early versions of *SimTower*, if you place anything—even open floor—on levels B8, B9, or B10 before placing the Metro Station, you are unable to place the station afterwards. This is true even if you first destroy all the properties you built on those three levels.

This problem seems buggy, since a Drug Store on level B9 at the far left side of your tower (in any reality, Sim or otherwise) should have no effect on the later construction of a Metro Station hundreds of yards away on the far right side of the tower. It doesn't interfere with the tunnel tube passage . . . and, in fact, you can build a Drug Store in that very same spot after you construct your Metro Station!

I'm not sure if this will be changed in later versions of the game. Just to be safe, don't build anything on the bottom three levels of your underground area until after you've constructed your Metro Station.

Cathedral

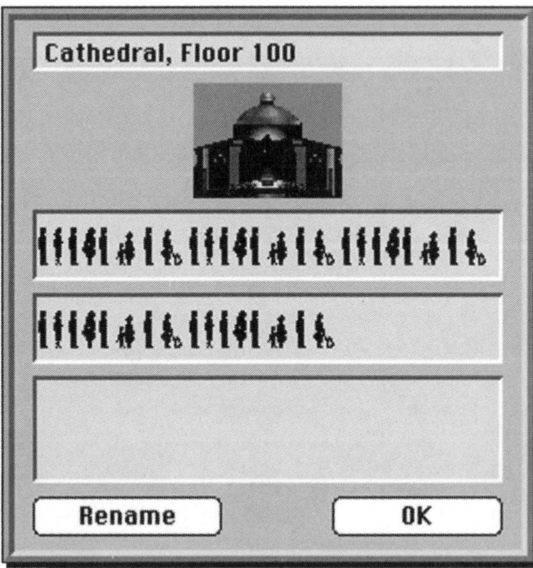

Figure 9-18.
Crown Your Tower.
This black-and-white screen shot does little justice to the grace and beauty of the *SimTower* Cathedral.

A five-star rating is a splendid achievement, one worthy of reward. And *SimTower's* reward indeed inspires awe. For $3,000,000 you can crown your towering achievement with a real jewel—a Cathedral on Floor 100.

Although the Cathedral appears to be open every day (lights on from 7:00 A.M. to 5:00 P.M.), Sims attend services only on weekends. Worshippers won't arrive until 9:00 A.M. The last Cathedral visitors leave around 1:00 P.M.

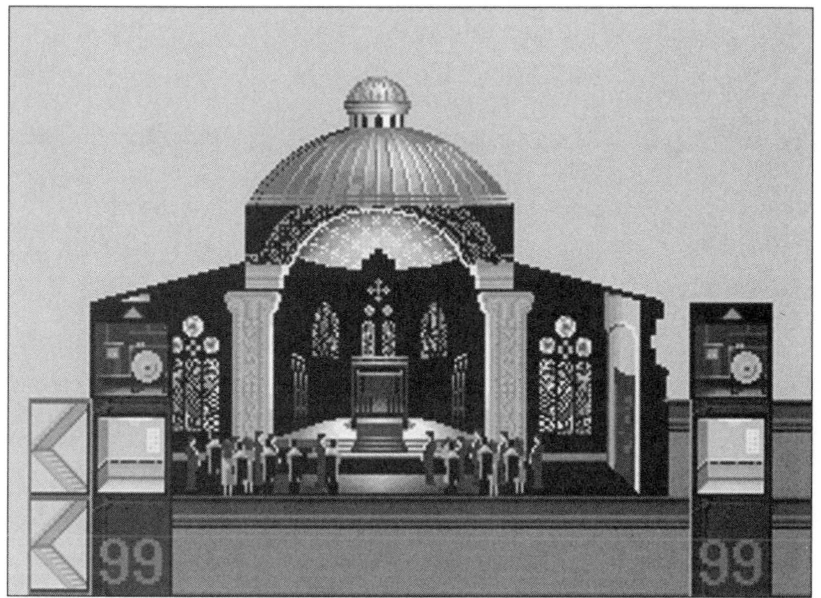

Figure 9-19.
Folks at Worship.
Weekends take on a spiritual aspect at the top of your tower. Keep an eye on the proceedings

PET
PET
74
73
72
69

10 Basement Levels

The area beneath your ground-floor lobby can be a veritable buzzing hive of activity. However, unlike your above-ground floors, your basement levels cannot support certain types of facilities. The chart below lists what you can and can't place underground in *SimTower*.

Tower Basement Levels	
Items Available	**Items Not Available**
All Elevators	Office
Fast Food	Condo
Restaurant	Hotel (Single, Twin, Suite)
Retail Shop	Lobby
Movie Theater	Cathedral (100th floor only)
Party Hall	
Housekeeping	
Security	
Medical Center	
Parking/Parking Ramp (basement only)	
Recycling Center (basement only)	
Metro Station (bottom 3 levels of basement only)	

Underground Transport

Express elevators stop at every floor once they get underground. Thus, with their wonderful double capacity (each Express car carries 42 passengers, versus only 21 passengers in a Standard car), they can service your entire underground complex with great efficiency.

Figure 10-1. Underground Complex. Here's a bustling, efficient tower basement. The Service elevator (left) bypasses rows of parking on levels B1 and B2 to connect the Recycling Centers with upper floors.

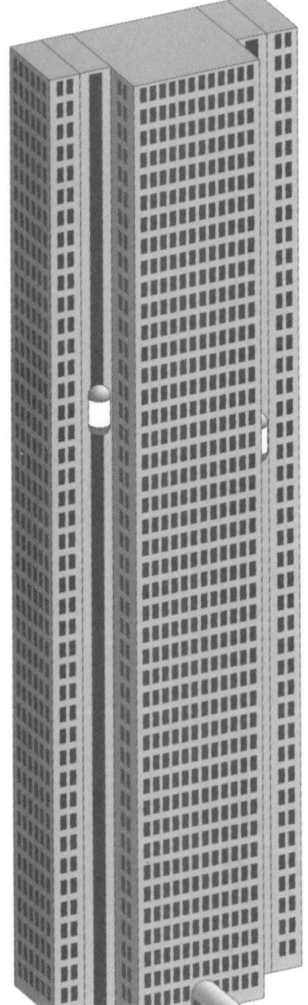

Figure 10-2. Underground Express. When you can afford it, drop a dedicated Express elevator down from the first floor lobby so that it services only your underground floors. You'll truly appreciate its double capacity. (Note that it bypasses the two floors of the Recycling Center.)

As soon as you can afford it, drop a couple of Express elevators down from the Floor 1 lobby to service your underground facilities. I've found that just two dedicated Express elevators (running underground only) can keep things moving briskly in my basement . . . even when I've developed everything from edge to edge in the entire underground area!

In the early stages of tower-building when money is more scarce, you should probably just install a Standard elevator shaft to get things flowing to the basement. But I highly recommend that you replace it with an Express elevator once you've built up both your star rating and your hoard of disposable income.

Run only Express elevators underground, if you can afford it.

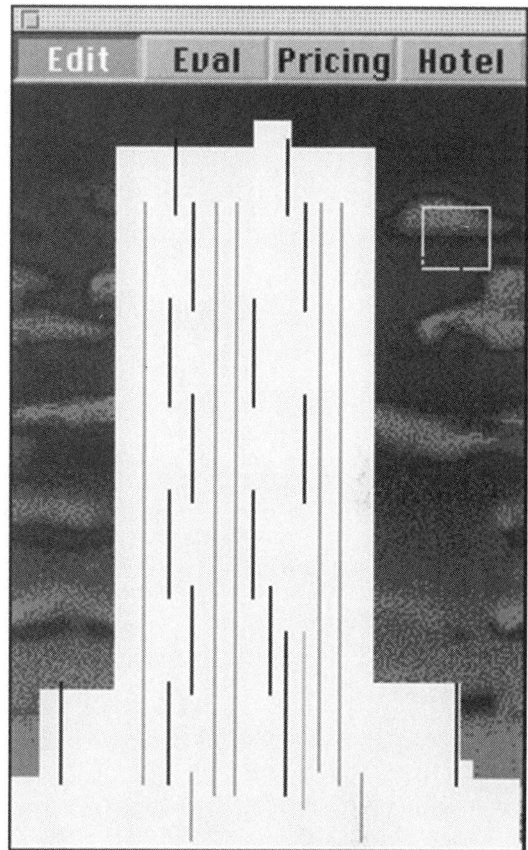

Figure 10-3.
Underground Express.
This map displays a tower with a fully developed underground area serviced by only two well-spaced Express elevators. They do the job quite well.

Recycling Efficiency

One other underground elevator note: If you reserve two upper-level basement floors for Recycling Centers only—that is, you put all Recycling Centers side-by-side in a horizontal row—you can then cancel Standard and Express elevator service to those floors. This reduces the elevator waiting time on other floors.

Remember, though: A Service elevator must run to at least one Recycling Center floor.

56
55
55
54
53
52
50
42
40

Part 3

Transportation

How to Keep Traffic Moving in a Complex Tower

11 Stairs, Escalators, and Elevators

If you read the message from Yoot Saito in the *SimTower* User's Manual from Maxis, you know that the whole *SimTower* concept evolved from his fascination with elevators. And if you've played *SimTower* at all before reading this book, you know that developing an effective transportation system easily comprises the most critical element of successful tower management.

This chapter examines each individual type of transportation device—Stairs, Escalators, and all three types of Elevators. In particular, it reviews the basic "hows" of transportation devices—how to place them and how they work. This chapter also describes the elevator control functions found in the Elevator Window. The next chapter discusses overall transportation strategy.

General Rules of Placement

Remember the Golden Rule of *SimTower*: Always plan ahead! If you just throw elevators hodgepodge into your tower without taking future growth considerations into account, you may find yourself blocked and frustrated later.

Placement strategy—where you put your elevators, stairs, and escalators in relation to each other—is very, very important in *SimTower*. This strategy is covered at length in the next chapter. For now, let's review four critical rules of transport placement.

Rule #1: A Sim can change elevators only ONCE per trip. It is important to remember this rule. Sims can transfer from a Standard elevator to another Standard elevator, or from a Standard elevator to an Express elevator (or vice-versa) in a single trip. But, again, no Sim can make more than one transfer per trip.

Rule #2: Sims can change elevators only on lobby floors. We've said it before in this book, and we'll say it again . . . and again and again. The only floors at which Sims can make an elevator transfer are floors 1, 15, 30, 45, 60, 75, and 90. And don't forget that an elevator transfer occurs only if you build lobbies on these floors.

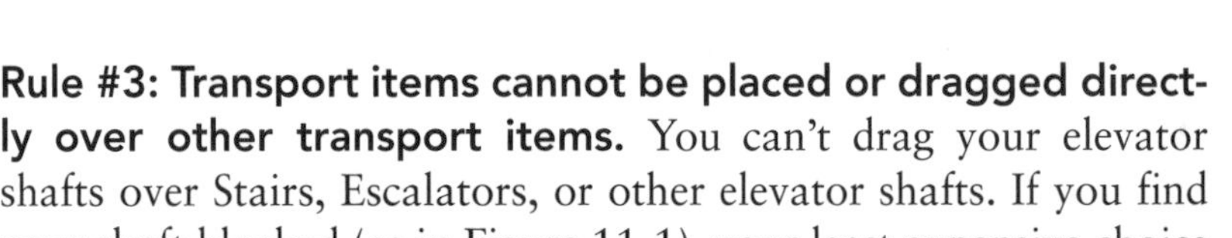

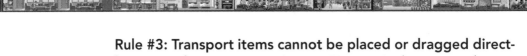

Rule #3: Transport items cannot be placed or dragged directly over other transport items. You can't drag your elevator shafts over Stairs, Escalators, or other elevator shafts. If you find your shaft blocked (as in Figure 11-1), your least expensive choice is to bulldoze the Stairs and/or Escalators, then rebuild them next to the elevator shaft after you've expanded it to the desired destination floor.

Figure 11-1. Blocked! Here's a bad situation. This elevator has no place to go. (Note the message in the Info Bar.) Fire up your bulldozer!

Rule #4: Elevator shafts cannot overlap unless they are at least eight floor sections apart. Interestingly, Stairs and Escalators are exactly eight floor sections wide. So, you can always fit a bank of Stairs or Escalators between two overlapping elevator shafts. (See Figure 11-2.) You can also use either your Stair tool or Escalator tool to measure exactly how close you can place a new elevator shaft next to an existing shaft.

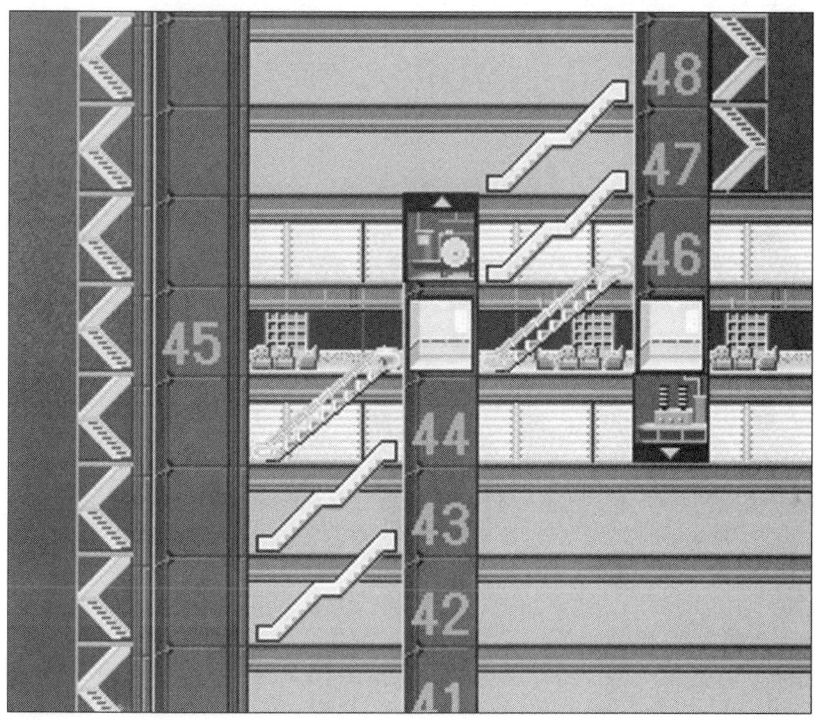

Figure 11-2. Elevator Spacing. Elevators must be at least eight floor units apart—the exact width of stairs and escalators.

Place Stairs and Escalators right next to elevator shafts. This maximizes the space available for future elevator shaft installments.

Stairs

Pretty tough to get excited about stairs, isn't it? OK, so maybe stair-climbing is great for the gluteal muscles. But extensive StairMaster conditioning belongs in a health club, not in your tower. This is transportation at its crudest and most low-tech—Sims pulled upward by their own hamstrings. Hey, even Cro-Magnon Man had that figured out.

Figure 11-3. Stairs.
A simple, crude traffic device. Placed wisely, stairs can ease the pressure on your elevator system.

Don't get me wrong. It doesn't hurt to connect certain floors with stairs. In fact, you can take a mighty load off of your elevator traffic with a couple of well-placed stairways. Example: By linking an all-Office floor and an adjacent Fast Food floor, you can reduce a lot of stress during lunch hour (12:00 - 1:00 P.M.).

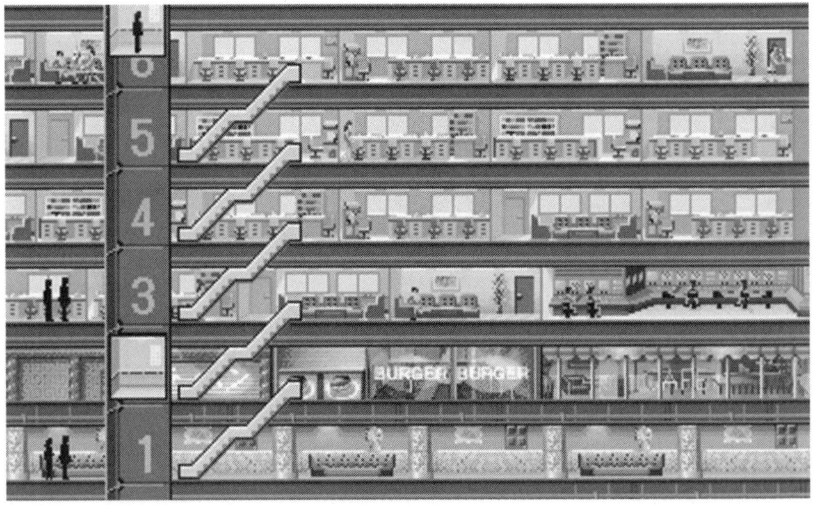

Figure 11-4. A Step Up.
Use Stairs to connect Office areas with Fast Food areas. It's also a good tactic to place Stairs right next to elevator shafts; that way, they're less likely to block the path of future shafts. (See Chapter 12 for more on this.)

But remember: *Sims won't take more than four flights of stairs in any one trip*. (Can you blame them? Sweating in a business suit really sucks.) And don't forget that Stairs and Escalators are considered the same type of item, and they're limited in number. You

Figure 11-5.
How Many on Board?
Click directly on Stairs in the Edit Window to get a current climber count.

can place a combined total of only 64 sets of Stairs and Escalators in any single tower. So every time you build a stairway, you reduce the number of Escalators you can build.

Overall, you need a lot of Escalators for an efficient transportation system. (More on this in the next section.) So, this brings up the question: Should you be conservative in the number of Stairs you place?

The answer: No. After all, until you earn a three-star rating, you don't have Escalators even available to you. Plus, Stairs are pretty cheap, costing a mere $5,000 apiece. Sprinkle them liberally around your tower at first. Focus on connecting Office floors with Fast Food areas. Later, as your rental income builds and your commercial zones develop, you can bulldoze many of your Stairs and build more Escalators.

Escalators

Nothing in life is more satisfying than walking up the down-escalator until mall cops get really ticked off and chase you away. Unfortunately, *SimTower* does not simulate this right-of-passage. However, Escalators do play a very important role in your tower traffic system. Without them, your commercial zones do meager business and tie up elevator traffic to boot.

Figure 11-6. Escalators. These mechanized movers provide a major key to the commercial health of your tower.

Escalators can link only commercial or public properties to one another. By "commercial," I mean shopping, dining, and entertainment properties. (See Chapter 8 for more on Commercial Zones.) By "public," I mean either a lobby or an open floor area.

In other words, you can use an Escalator to link the following:

- Two commercial properties
- Commercial property to a lobby or open floor area
- Two open floor areas
- Lobby to an open floor area

If you try to place an Escalator on a spot where either its top or bottom touches an Office, Condo, Hotel room, Parking area, or tower facility (Security, Medical, Housekeeping, Recycling, etc.), you hear an annoying click and your Info bar flashes the message shown in Figure 11-7.

There are two other things to remember about Escalator travel. First, Sims can take no more than seven Escalators per trip.

Figure 11-7. Take Your Escalator Elsewhere, Bub. The message suggests you get thee to a commercial space, but it doesn't have to be commercial, actually. For example . . .

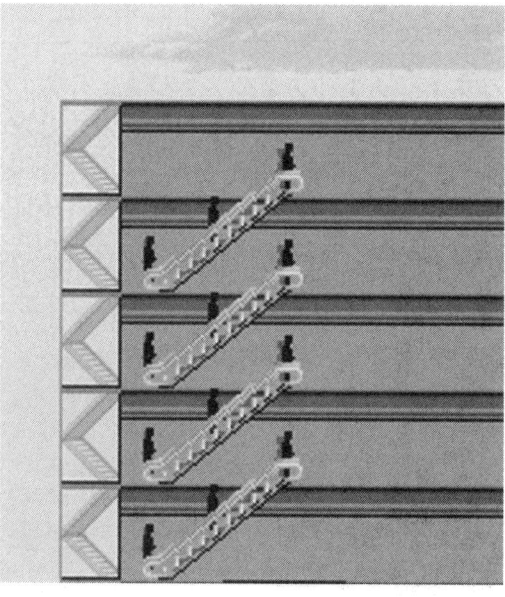

Figure 11-8. . . . you can link open spaces with Escalators, too. Here, I just built empty floor space at the top of my tower. The escalators dropped in nicely, without a whimper of protest.

Second, there is no waiting to get on an Escalator. Escalator strategy is discussed in depth in Chapter 12. For now, just note that it is an excellent idea to link all floors in your tower's commercial zones with Escalators.

Elevators

SimTower's elevator system looks awfully complex. The first time you open an Elevator Window and see all those buttons and dots and triangles and little clockfaces and such—well, it can be pretty frightening. (That's why you bought this book, right?)

Actually, *SimTower's* elevator operation is only as complex as you want to make it. In fact, you can set up an efficient elevator system quite simply, without a lot of experimenting, back-checking, adjusting, tweaking, and so forth. Before you get into scheduling strategies and optimal control settings, though—which is covered in Chapter 12—take a little time to review the basic how-tos of elevator placement.

Basic Elevator Facts

Let's review a few facts about elevators.

1. Each elevator shaft can hold up to eight cars.
2. Standard and Service elevators can stretch 30 floors, top to bottom.
3. Express elevators can run from the very bottom of the tower (B9) to the very top (Floor 100)—if there are no other transport items blocking the way.
4. Express elevators stop every 15 floors above the ground-level lobby—on 15, 30, 45, 60, 75, and 90. Below ground, they stop on every floor, B1 through B9. (Floor B10 is reserved for your Metro tunnel.)
5. No elevator can extend above Floor 100 or below Floor B9.
6. Elevator shafts cannot overlap, unless they are a horizontal distance of eight floor sections or more away from each other.
7. Sims can change elevators only on lobby floors and only once per trip.
8. Sims waiting on the left side of the elevator shaft have requested a car going up; Sims on the right side are waiting for a car going down.

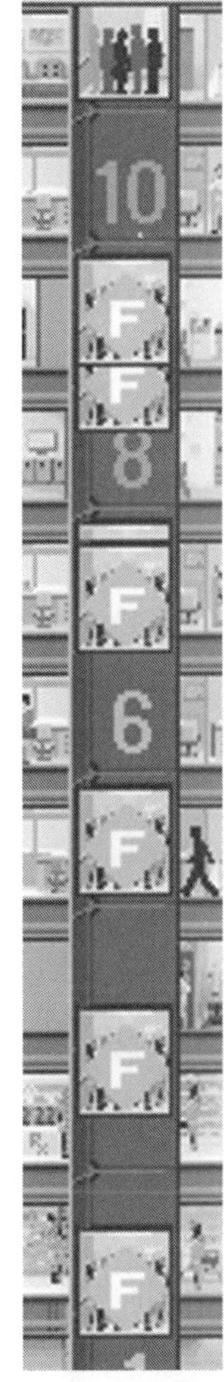

Figure 11-9. Busy Shaft.
A full, active tower puts a heavy load on your elevator system. Can you control your traffic?

How to Add an Elevator

To place an elevator, take the following steps.

1. Click and hold on the Tool Bar Elevator icon. This opens a drop-down menu.
2. Drag the mouse pointer down to highlight the icon for the type of elevator (Standard, Service, or Express) that you wish to place.
3. Release the mouse button to select the desired elevator tool.
4. Move the mouse pointer onto the main window. Your mouse pointer assumes the size and shape of the selected elevator tool.
5. Place the elevator tool on the desired spot in your tower, then click to place an elevator shaft.

The new shaft includes a single elevator car. The floor on which you first place your shaft becomes the "waiting floor" of the first car. For more information on what this means, see the next section, Waiting Floors.

6. Select the Finger icon from the Tool Bar.
7. Click and hold on the small triangle at the top or bottom of the elevator, then drag it up or down to extend the elevator to the desired length.

Figure 11-10. After you place your elevator shaft in the desired place (left), use the Finger to drag it up or down to the desired height (right).

Remember, you cannot drag the elevator shaft over other transport items. If Stairs, Escalators, or other elevator shafts block the planned extension of your new elevator shaft, you face a bad situation. Your only choices are to (1) destroy the blocking items and replace them elsewhere; (2) destroy the elevator you just placed and replace it elsewhere; or (3) accept the limitations of your stunted elevator shaft. Obviously, none of these are attractive alternatives.

To add another car to the shaft, take the following steps.

1. Repeat steps 1-3, above, to activate the appropriate Elevator tool.
2. Move the cursor to the Edit Window.
3. Click on the floor of the elevator shaft on which you wish to place the new car.

NOTE You can place a new car on any floor of an elevator shaft.

Waiting Floors

When you place a new car in an elevator shaft, the floor on which you placed it automatically becomes the "waiting" floor for that car. This means that when the car is not in use, it returns to that floor and waits until it is summoned. Waiting floors are indicated by pink numbers on visible elevator shafts.

For more on waiting floors—particularly, to learn how to change waiting floors—see the next section, Elevator Window.

Figure 11-11.
Elevator Window.
Click on an open section of elevator shaft . . . and there it is, the scariest-looking thing in *SimTower.*

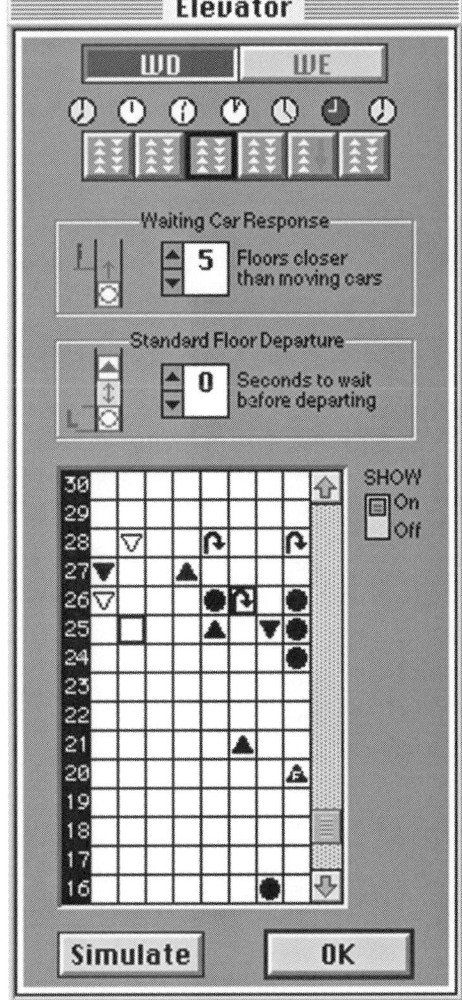

Elevator Window

Each elevator shaft in *SimTower* displays in an Elevator Window its own specific operating information. To access the Elevator Window, click the Magnifying Glass tool on any unoccupied spot on the elevator shaft. Note that the key word here is unoccupied. If you click on one of the elevator cars in the shaft, you get a Facility Window with information on that particular car, as in Figure 11-12.

NOTE If the Show button is off (see Show Button, below), the shaft itself is no longer visible; clicking on it produces no result. To open the Elevator Window in this case, click the Magnifying Glass tool on the elevator mechanism square at the top or bottom tip of the shaft.

The first thing to catch your eye in the Elevator Window is the grid box in the bottom half of the window. Numbers on the left side of the grid represent the floors serviced by the elevator shaft. Each vertical column of boxes represents the path of one of the cars in the shaft. All those little geometrical figures—triangles, squares, circles, curved arrows, etc.—are symbols that represent car movements in the shaft.

Figure 11-12. Car Info. If you click on a car instead of an open shaft, you get the Facility Window with information on that specific car.

NOTE To cancel service to a particular floor in a shaft, click on the floor number either in the Elevator Window (which puts a red X through the cancelled floor) or on the shaft itself (which makes the floor number disappear). Remember, you can not cancel service to a waiting floor.

Car Movement Symbols

When you open your Elevator Window, you see a lot of little symbols appearing and disappearing and moving up and down the vertical columns of the grid box. These represent the position, movement, and destination of the elevator cars in that particular shaft.

Remember, each vertical column represents the path of one car in the shaft. Therefore, all of the symbols in a single column refer to the movements and destinations of a single car.

The table on the following page lists the meaning of all car movement symbols.

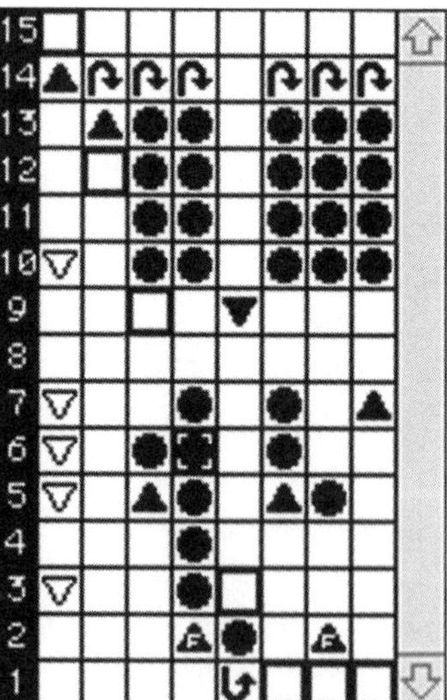

Figure 11-13. Geometry in Motion. Here's a rush hour look at the Elevator Window grid box. What does it all mean?

▼ **Active car** points in current direction of movement

▼ **Full car** points in current direction of movement

▽ **Service call** points in direction waiting passenger wants to go

☐ **"Waiting" floor**

☐ **Idle car** waiting for service call at "waiting" floor

● **Destination** for passenger in active car

↱ **Floor** where active car will stop and reverse directions

Show Button

Just to the right of the box grid is an on/off button labeled Show. When the button is on, the elevator shaft represented by the Elevator Window is fully visible (as in Figure 11-14). When the Show button is switched off, the shaft turns transparent, with only its cars and an outline of the shaft visible (as in Figure 11-15).

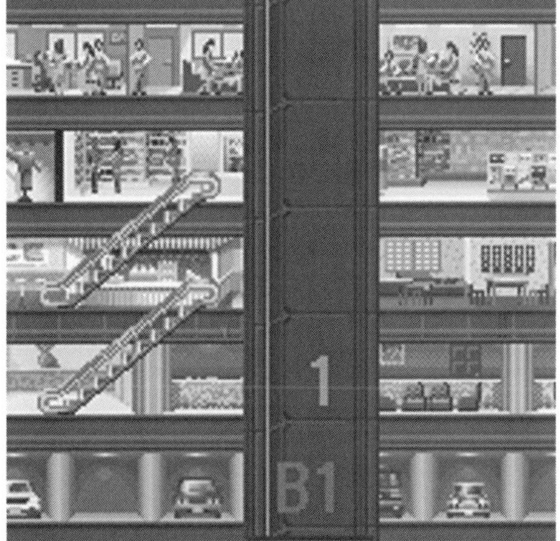

Figure 11-14. Show Your Shaft. When the Show button is on, the corresponding elevator shaft is fully visible.

Figure 11-15. Hide Your Shaft. When the Show button is off, the corresponding elevator shaft turns transparent, leaving visible only the cars and an outline of the shaft.

How to Change Waiting Floors

As you'll see in the next chapter, assigning waiting floors to elevator cars is an important part of elevator strategy. When you install a new car in an elevator shaft, the floor you clicked on becomes the car's waiting floor. Waiting floors are indicated by pink numbers in the shaft.

But how do you change an elevator car's waiting floor? The answer: It has to be done in the Elevator Window.

To change an elevator car's waiting floor, take the following steps.

1. Open the Elevator Window.
2. Find the floor number (on the left side of the grid box) of the car's current waiting floor.
3. Follow the row of boxes horizontally from the floor number until you find one outlined by a bold "waiting box" (see diagram in Car Movement Symbols, above). This box is in the vertical column of the car you want to change.
4. Now move the cursor up or down that car's column to the desired waiting floor, then click in that floor's box.

You have now changed that car's waiting floor. If the car is idle, it immediately moves to the new waiting floor. (See Figures 11-16, 11-17, and 11-18.)

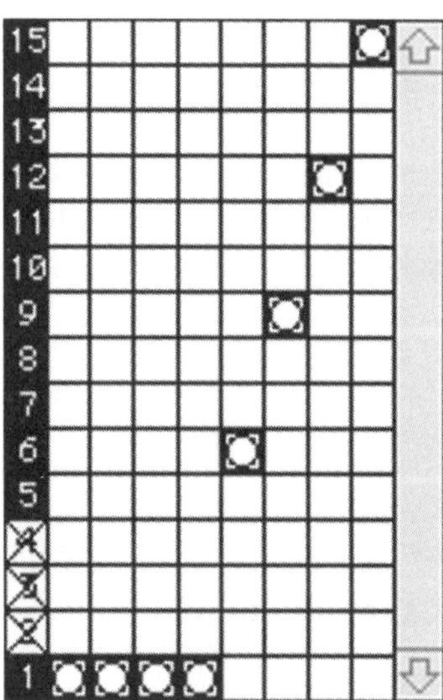

Figure 11-16. How to Change Waiting Floors
In this shot, your waiting cars are spread nicely along the shaft, as the "waiting boxes" show you. But suppose you want them all waiting on the Floor 1 lobby for the morning rush.

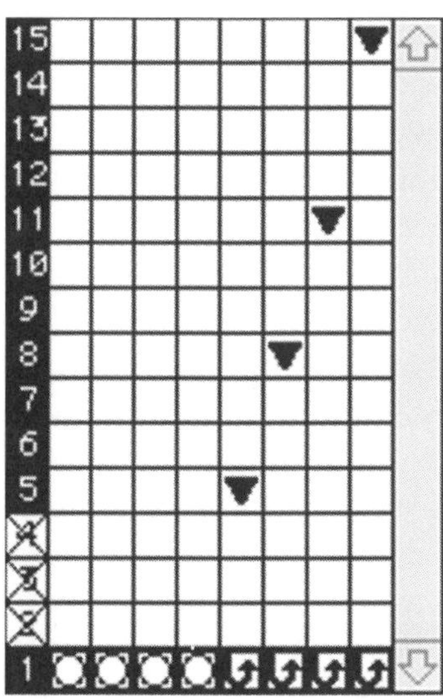

Figure 11-17.
Click the cursor on the Floor 1 row of all columns that represent cars with higher waiting floors—in this case, the four columns from the right half of the grid box. The "waiting boxes" for all four cars hop down to Floor 1, and the cars begin to move down to their new waiting floors (as indicated by the black triangles pointing down).

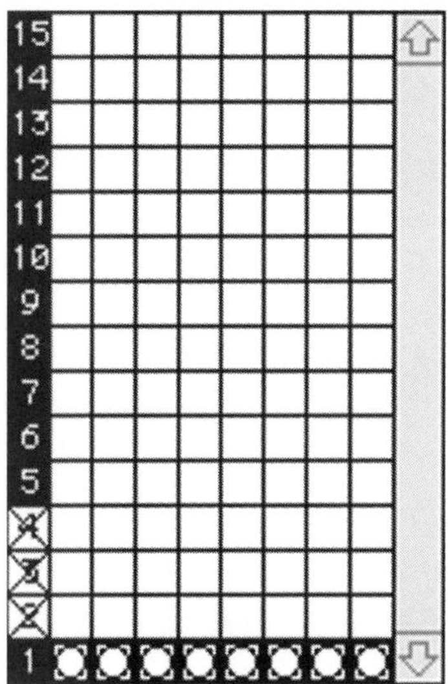

Figure 11-18.
Now your ducks are all in a row. Bring on the morning rush!

Car Regulation

The top half of the Elevator Window features four sets of controls: Weekday-Weekend (WD-WE) buttons; Waiting Car Response control; Standard Floor Departure control; and Custom Time Period control. Each of these controls regulate some aspect of your elevator's operating system.

Weekday-Weekend Buttons

Figure 11-19.
Weekday-Weekend Buttons.
You can have completely different control settings for weekdays (WD) and weekends (WE). Click the appropriate button to display and change settings.

As in the real world, *SimTower's* weekdays and weekends feature very different patterns of activity. *SimTower* lets you address these differences with the pair of buttons at the very top of the Elevator Window.

When the WD button is pushed, all of the settings in the Elevator Window apply to *SimTower's* two weekdays (1st WD and 2nd WD). When the WE button is pushed, all of the settings in the Elevator Window apply to *SimTower's* single weekend day (WE). Changes made in the weekend (WE) control settings do not affect weekday (WD) control settings for that elevator shaft, and vice versa.

Waiting Car Response

Here's an interesting little control device. The Waiting Car Response box regulates how responsive your elevator cars are to service requests. Example: Let's say the number in the Waiting Car Response box is five (5), the default setting. A Sim hits the button on Floor 82 to summon an elevator. *SimTower's* elevator system automatically looks to first call moving cars. However, if a non-moving car is five floors (or more) closer than the nearest car in motion, the non-moving car answers the call.

So, if the nearest moving car is up on Floor 89 and a car sits idle on Floor 85 (only four floors closer), the moving car answers the call. But if the idle car waits on 84, it is now five floors closer than the moving car, and it answers the call.

You might wonder why anyone would set the Waiting Car Response number high, thus effectively immobilizing idle cars if other cars are in motion. One reason is to keep certain cars at their waiting floors, because those floors have high traffic concentrations. But then you run the risk of making Sims turn red, because a couple of overworked moving cars keep canceling out idle cars that sit just a floor or two away from the angry Sims. I've seen it happen in my towers, and it is exasperating.

My advice here: Always set the Waiting Car Response number to one (1) in every shaft.

Figure 11-20. Waiting Car Response. Do you want to keep cars loyal to their waiting floors? Raise the response number. Do you want cars responsive to service requests anywhere along the shaft? Lower the response number.

NOTE

When you change the Waiting Car Response number, that change applies only to the time period during which you made the change. Whenever *SimTower* moves into a new time period, the Waiting Car Response number for all cars in the shaft reverts to the default number, which is five. You have to reset it for each time period. (For a listing and description of the six *SimTower* time periods, see Custom Time Period Controls on page 105.)

Standard Floor Departure

The Standard Floor Departure control lets you decide how long elevator cars pause before leaving a floor. Most of the time, you want to leave this at its default setting of "0 Seconds to wait before departing." Occasionally—during a heavy rush hour, for example—

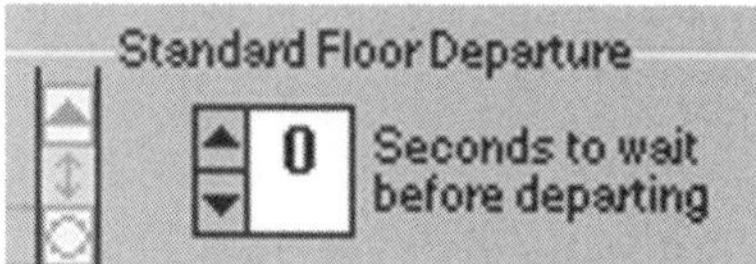

Figure 11-21. Standard Floor Departure. Click on the arrows to increase or decrease the amount of time your elevator cars pause at each floor before departing.

you may find that pausing a couple of seconds helps fill up cars with late-arriving passengers. But my advice is this: The precious seconds spent waiting are rarely worth it.

Custom Time Period Controls

The flow of traffic through your *SimTower* varies throughout the day, from beginning to end. As in real life, there is ebb and flow, peak and valley. Above all, there is rush hour. One feature of your Elevator Window is the ability to add certain "express" functions to your elevators at certain times of the day.

See that row of seven tiny clocks across the top of the window? Note that each is set to a particular time of day. Below the clocks is a row of six buttons. Each button is positioned between a corresponding pair of clocks just above it. That's because each button sets a custom elevator movement pattern for the period of time between the times listed on the two clockfaces.

The clockfaces are small and a bit hard to read, so here are the time periods represented by each pair, from left to right.

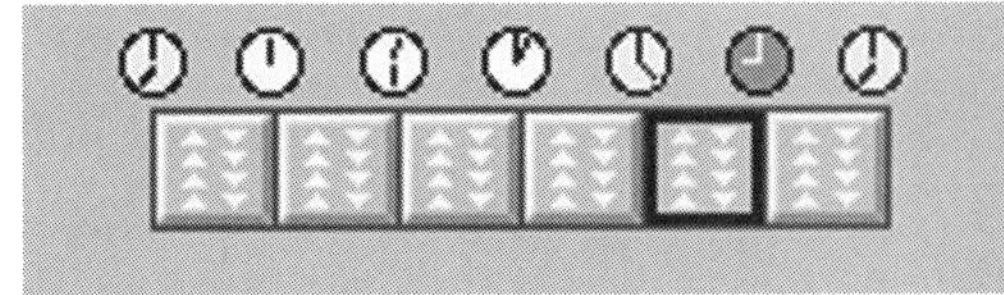

Figure 11-22. Custom Time Period Controls. Here's where you customize your elevator movements for different time periods of each day—morning rush, lunch hour, afternoon rush, etc.

7:00 A.M.-12:00 P.M. (noon) — Morning rush hour begins at 7:00 A.M. and intensifies at about 9:00 A.M. During that time, Office people all go up, Hotel and Condo people go down. At 10:00 A.M., shops and fast food places open. Shoppers and diners from outside begin to head up the tower, and Office workers take coffee breaks and early lunch.

12:00-12:30 P.M. — Total madness. (Watch the clock in your Info bar slow to a crawl.) Together with the half-hour period that follows, this is the most hectic traffic period of the day. Everybody goes to lunch—outsiders come in, insiders go out (or stay in).

12:30-1:00 P.M. — As in the previous half-hour, all is chaos. Toward the end of this period, lunching workers swarm to the elevators to return to their Offices by 1:00 P.M. Lobbies and fast food floors jam with elevator passengers.

1:00-5:00 P.M. — Eye of the hurricane. This lull between the lunch and going-home rush hours features a moderate increase in shopping traffic due to the first movie showing of the day (1:00 - 4:00 P.M.). Otherwise, things remain calm until 5 o'clock.

5:00-9:00 P.M. — And home they go! The afternoon rush is heaviest from 5:00 P.M. to about 7:00 P.M., because not only do you have Office Sims heading home, you also have Hotel visitors checking in. This can make it difficult to regulate elevator flow.

9:00 P.M.-7:00 A.M. — Aside from residual rush-hour folks and some light restaurant traffic, this is rest time for your poor, overworked elevators. If your tower is huge, you may have minor activity well into the wee morning hours. But most towers fall asleep by midnight or 1:00 A.M.

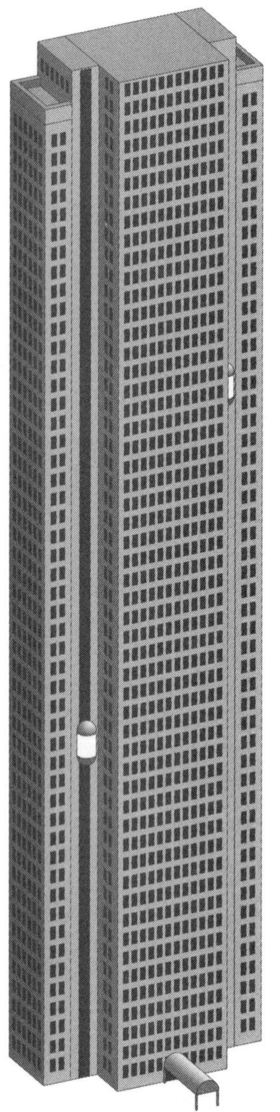

Figure 11-23. Custom Buttons.
Here's the drop-down menu listing the three types of elevator movement patterns you can choose for each time period.

Click each button to reveal a drop-down menu with your three choices of elevator movement patterns—Local, Express to Top, and Express to Bottom (see Figure 11-23). Remember that your choice applies to all cars in the elevator shaft during the selected time period. Unfortunately, you cannot program individual cars.

Local (the default choice) directs all elevator cars in the shaft to respond to the nearest service calls and to carry passengers to their destinations, moving up and down without restrictions.

Express to Top directs cars to pick up passengers floor-by-floor as they head down . . . but when these cars reverse directions to go up, they do not stop until they reach the highest floor in that shaft. Passengers who want to travel just a few floors up may have to ride clear to the top, then ride back down floor-by-floor until the elevator reaches their destination.

Express to Bottom directs cars to pick up passengers floor-by-floor as they head up . . . but when these cars reverse directions to go down, they do not stop until they reach the lowest floor in that shaft. Passengers who want to travel just a few floors down may have to ride clear to the bottom, then ride back up floor-by-floor until the elevator reaches their destination.

56
55
55
52
50
42
40

12 Transit Systems

A *SimTower* skyscraper, especially a big one, is a small city. It includes everything—home, business, shopping, dining, entertainment, hotel, hospital, security—all wrapped up in a nice, neat box. But, as in a city, everything must be connected. Think of tower inhabitants as commuters without cars, trains, or buses. The key to success in *SimTower* consists of maintaining good traffic flow. And the key to good traffic flow is understanding how individual transportation devices can work together to form efficient transit systems.

This chapter covers where to place Stairs, Escalators, and all three types of elevators. But first, it opens with a discussion of what I consider the most important aspect of any successful mega-tower development—the elevator/escalator interplay in your commercial zones.

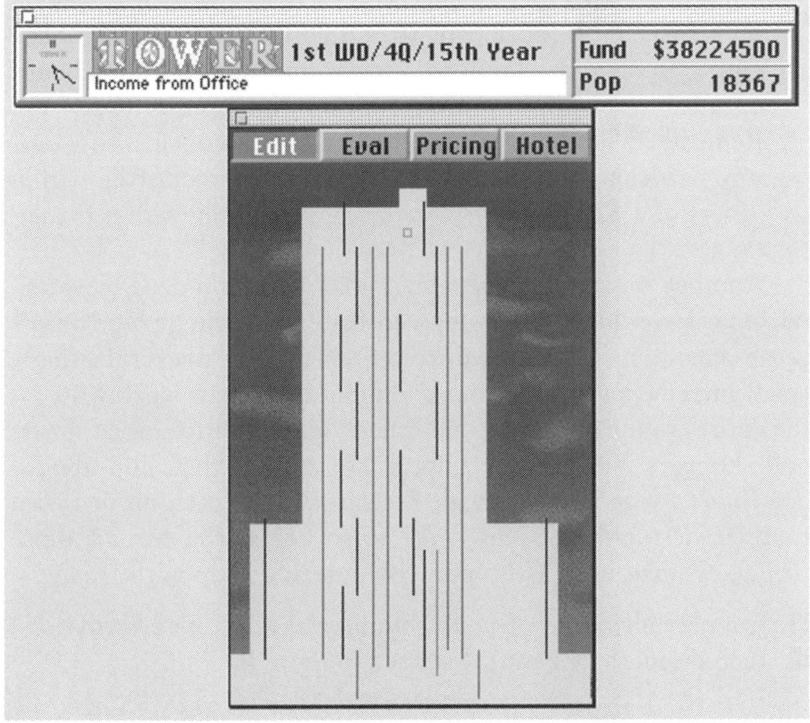

Figure 12-1. Mega-Tower. Only 15 years old, yet this huge, hunkering beast boasts a cash fund of $38 million and nearly obliterates the entire map screen. Big towers depend on efficient transit systems for their health. Note the staggered elevators, most of which span only far enough to connect successive Sky Lobbies.

Elevator/Escalator Interplay

If you developed your commercial zones according to the strategies recommended in Chapter 8, you should have constructed clusters of commercial tenants within five floors (up or down) of your Sky Lobbies. This is the zone where shops, food, and entertainment properties thrive. The problem is, when they thrive, they clog your elevators.

Relief is available, however, and it's spelled E-S-C-A-L-A-T-O-R. You can make your entire system of elevators considerably more efficient and speedy by taking two simple steps.

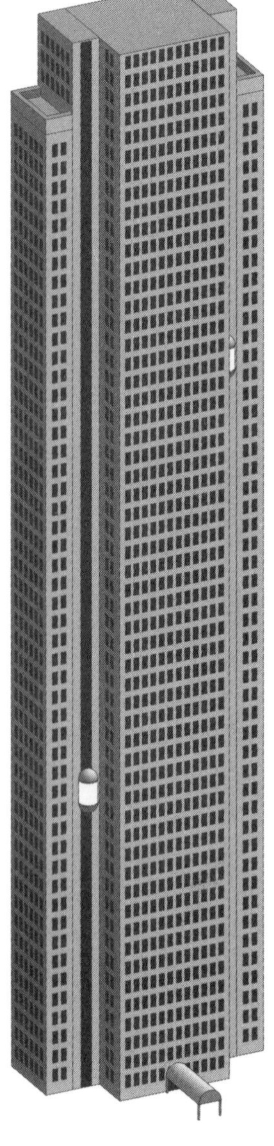

1. Use Escalators to link each Sky Lobby with all of the commercial floors clustered above and below it.
2. Deactivate all elevator floor service to those commercial floors.

What happens when you do this?

First of all, you eliminate an entire category of passenger from your Standard elevators. "Outside" Sims always flock into your tower to shop, dine, and see movies in your commercial zones. With this new setup, they ride Express elevators up to Sky Lobbies . . . then, instead of transferring to Standard elevators to complete the journey to commercial floor destinations, they just hop aboard Escalators.

Remember, Sims may take up to seven Escalators in a row during any particular trip. Since commercial tenants must be within five floors of a Sky Lobby to thrive, they are easily within Escalator range.

Another outstanding benefit is that your Standard elevators make far fewer lunch hour stops. Instead of shuttling your tower's lunch-and-shop Office crowd from floor-to-floor in excruciatingly small increments of movement, Standard cars can jet down past the entire commercial zone and quickly dump Office-based diners and shoppers into the Sky Lobby. Those folks then hop aboard *SimTower's* wonderful no-wait Escalators and zoom up or down to their destinations. This same logic holds true for all those Condo Woman-with-Kid types who dine and shop in the tower.

TIP Connect all floors of your commercial areas with escalators, then discontinue elevator service to those floors.

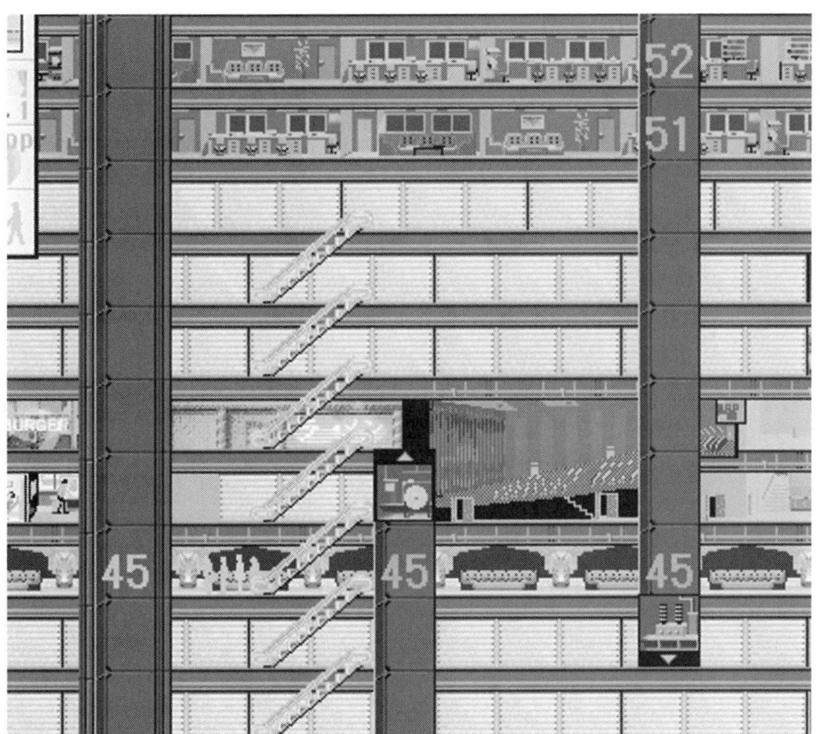

Figure 12-2. How Escalators Relieve Elevator Traffic. This commercial area is bustling, thanks to the smooth interplay between elevators (both Standard and Express) and escalators. Note how Standard elevator service to commercial floors 46-50 has been eliminated (far right); escalators running up from the Sky Lobby (Floor 45) make elevator service to those floors unnecessary.

Where to Place Transit Items

As stated in the last chapter, it's good to plan ahead, rather than let things expand haphazardly. Hey, life is like that. So is real estate—whether urban or suburban, horizontal or vertical, virtual or actual. Plugging elevators into your tower on an ad hoc basis may work out okay in small structures. But as you expand, you'll find that you can quite easily blunder into inefficient transit patterns.

Spacing Concerns: Width

I've said this before, but here it goes again: When placing elevator shafts, it's very important to remember that you cannot expand one shaft past another, unless you have at least eight floor sections of space between them—the exact width of a set of Stairs or Escalators.

This becomes particularly important when placing a new Express elevator in a fairly tall tower. Before construction, you should always scroll up the proposed Express path to the top of

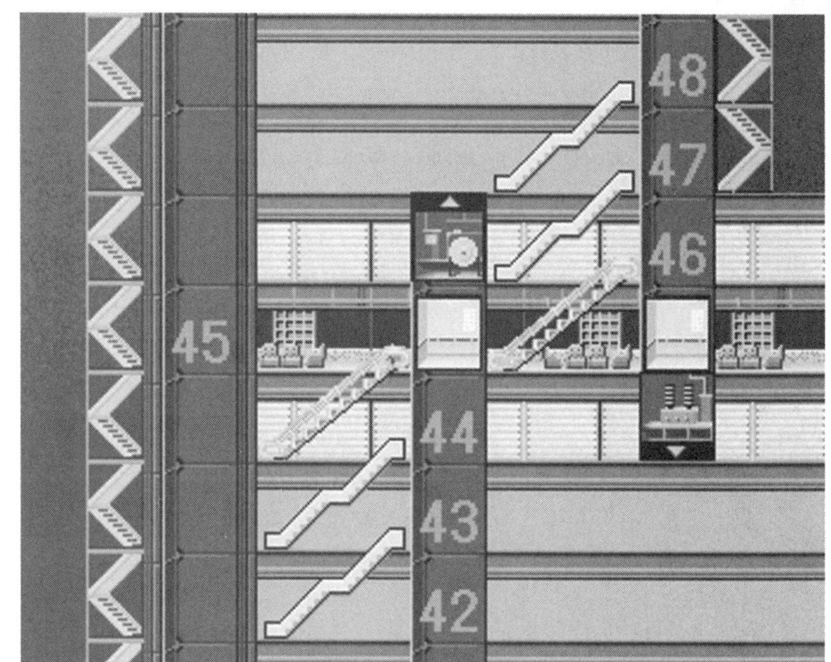

Figure 12-3. Elevator Spacing. Elevators must be at least eight floor sections apart in order to overlap—the exact width of both Escalators and Stairs, as seen here.

Figure 12-4. Not a Pretty Picture. You placed that brand new Express elevator without scrolling up to check for other shafts . . . and look what happened.

the tower and verify that none of your upper-floor elevator shafts are within eight floor sections of that path.

For this same reason, it's also a good idea to place Escalators and Stairs right next to elevator shafts, especially on upper floors. Suppose you want to drop in a new Express elevator shaft later. If you've placed it so that you have the required cushion of eight floor sections to expand past upper-floor shafts, then you won't run into any Escalators or Stairs either, since they fit into that eight-section cushion. Nothing is more exasperating than saving up the $400,000 for that Express elevator you so desperately need, plugging it into Floor 1, expanding it upward . . . then getting blocked by scatterings of Stairs and Escalators placed thoughtlessly in your upper floors.

Spacing Concerns: Height

Standard elevators can expand 30 floors in height. But with only eight cars, an elevator shaft spread over 30 very busy floors can easily get overtaxed. Feedback from *SimTower* fanatics has produced a nearly unanimous strategy tip: Run your Standard elevators no further than from one Sky Lobby to the next — a length of only 16 floors.

Use Express elevators to move your Sims over long distances to higher levels. I highly recommend that you build plenty of Express shafts—at least four or five running to the top of large towers, plus two for servicing underground floors only. (More on this in the next section.) Remember, Express cars have twice the capacity of Standard cars (42 to 21), so you want to funnel as much traffic into them as possible. If you've connected your commercial zones with Escalators and blanked out the commercial floors on your Standard elevators (as described in the Elevator/Escalator Interplay section, above), your Express elevators can handle a very large percentage of your tower's traffic volume.

Of course, you are limited to a total of 24 elevator shafts. So, it is possible to run out of elevators in a really huge tower. If this happens, you may need to bulldoze some of your Standard elevators, move them out horizontally into new tower wings, or perhaps even expand them to a full 30 floors. But I would avoid this as much as possible.

Check out my massive masterpiece in Figure 12-5. Only two of my 16 Standard Elevators extend a full 30 floors. The other 14

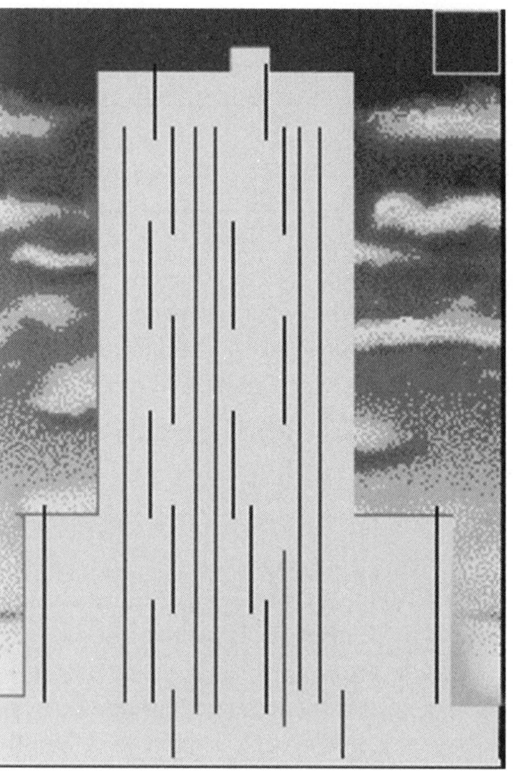

Figure 12-5.
Mega-Tower Revisited.
Here's a nice, thick, juicy piece of 100-story tower. Note how the Standard elevators are staggered in pairs, each running only from one Sky Lobby to the next (except for the two out on the wings). Five Express elevators run to the top of the building; two others service underground floors only.

are short and very efficient, linking lobbies and extending no more than 16 floors apiece.

TIP: Whenever your tower grows to a new Sky Lobby level, build the lobby as soon as possible, then immediately expand all of your Express elevators up to it.

Underground Elevators

Express elevators, you may notice, stop at every underground floor, from B1 down to B9. With their big-capacity cars (42 passengers versus only 21 in Standard elevators), they make very nice underground shuttles. As soon you can afford it, drop a new Express shaft from the first floor lobby down to the bottom of the basement. (Don't extend it any higher than Floor 1.) It becomes particularly welcome once you've built your Metro Station.

Of course, since Express elevator shafts cost twice as much as Standard elevator shafts ($400,000 versus $200,000), you might want to drop a Standard shaft down into the basement levels at

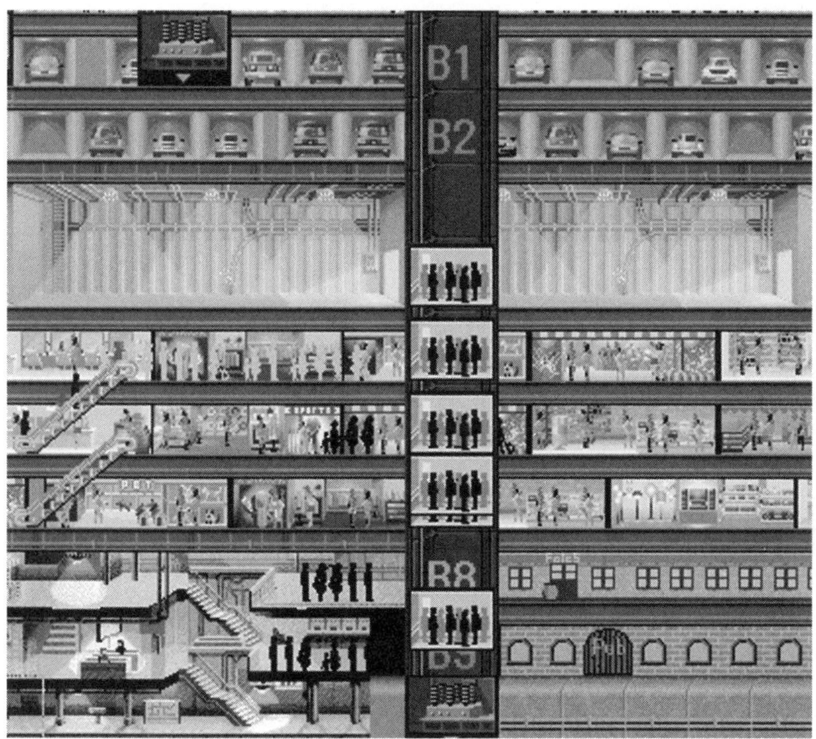

Figure 12-6. Underground Workhorse. Just two of these heavy-duty Express elevators (running from the Floor 1 lobby down to Level B9) can handle the traffic in your entire underground complex . . . even if every square inch is fully developed!

first when money is scarce. You can always replace it with an Express shaft later when your working fund is a bit more ample.

TIP Keep elevator service to underground floors separate from service to upper floors.

Placing Service Elevators

Service elevators provide service to Hotel floors and your Recycling Center complex. Since Service elevators carry only garbage and a few housekeepers, and they count against your limit of 24 elevator shafts, you want as few of them as possible. As your tower grows, Express and Standard elevators become much more valuable.

Here's a big strategy tip: Build your hotel floors low on your tower (no higher than Floor 25 or so) and make sure that at least one of your contiguous Recycling Centers resides on an upper basement floor (no lower than level B3 or so). If you do that, you'll find that a single Service elevator is all you need for the entire building!

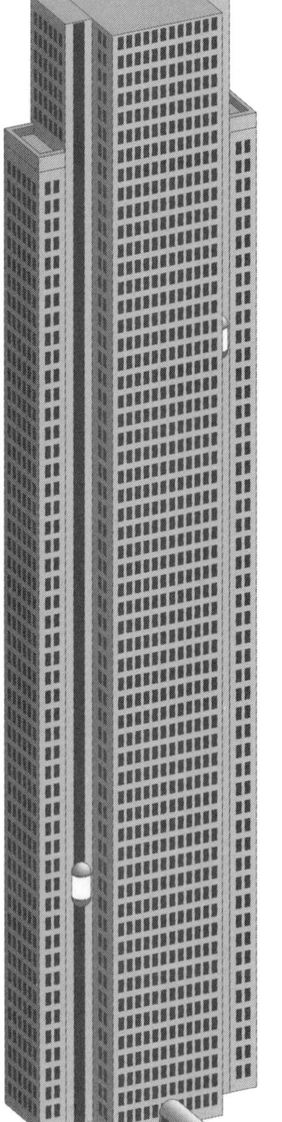

Figure 12-7.
Don't Waste Elevators!
Build your highest Hotel level on Floor 25 or lower. Then a single Service elevator can reach the top of your Hotel zone . . .

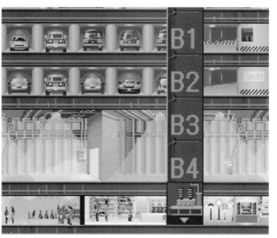

Figure 12-8.
. . . yet still reach down to your Recycling Center complex at its bottom level.

Service To Recycling Centers

Service elevators must run to at least one level of your Recycling Centers. A single service elevator will service that Recycling Center and all other Recycling Centers connected to it, even if they are stacked vertically. (See Figures 12-9 and 12-10.)

Figure 12-9.
If you place all your Recycling Centers adjacent to one another (as in the L-shaped configuration, above), you can run a Service elevator to just one of them and get service to all of them. Here, the elevator stops at only one level (B3) of the recycling complex, yet . . .

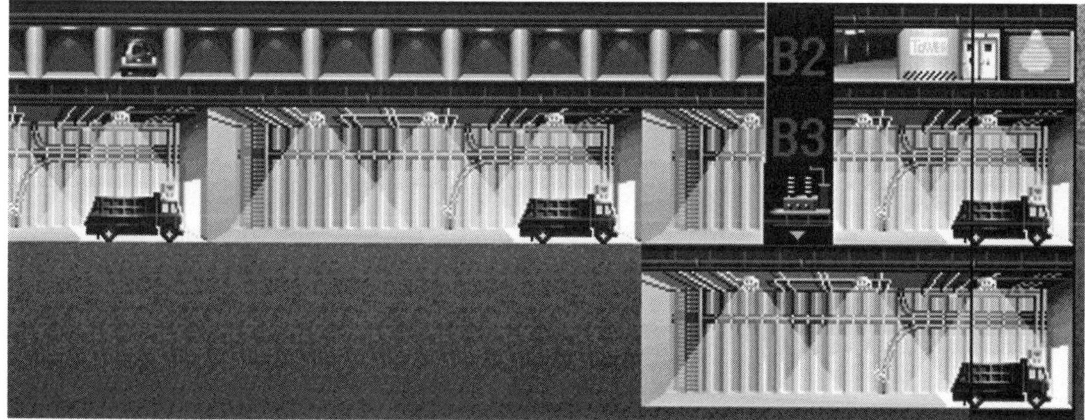

Figure 12-10.
. . . it still services all of the adjacent Recycling Centers.

Elevator Scheduling

As you know, *SimTower* gives you a remarkable amount of control over your elevator operating systems. However, let me say this: I've spent hours and hours experimenting with *SimTower's* elevators. I've talked to testers, producers, and other *SimTower* fanatics via phone, fax, Internet—sometimes even resorting to the primitive communications mode of speaking face-to-face. We've discussed

SimTower elevator strategy ad nauseum. And the consensus position on elevator settings is kind of surprising.

It is this: Despite all the controls and buttons, there is really only one optimal setting—for all elevators, at all times of the day, in all zoning situations. That's right . . . one setting for all situations.

I call it the Universal Setting. You'll find it in Figure 12-11.

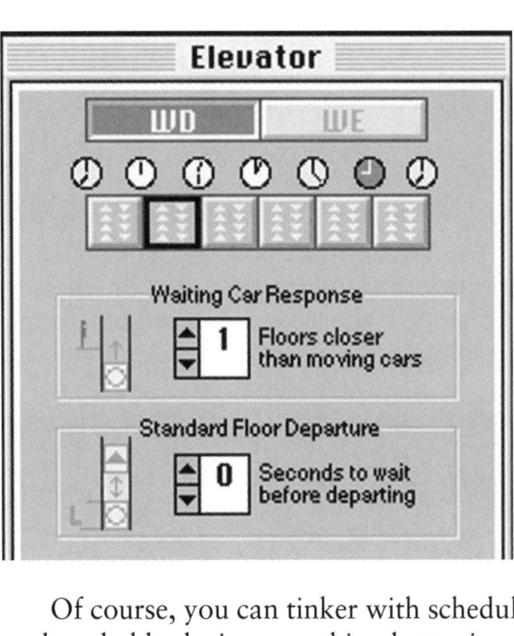

Figure 12-11. Universal Setting. Leave the Custom Time Period control set to Local for all time periods and keep Standard Floor Departure at 0, but drop Waiting Car Response to one (1). Voila. All situations handled, efficiently.

Of course, you can tinker with scheduling for hours, like I did, and probably devise something better in specific situations. But in most cases, the increase in traffic flow efficiency is so small, it's hardly worth the effort. In any case, using the Universal Setting lets you focus on zoning, pricing, and evaluation strategies, which are far trickier and ultimately, more time-consuming than elevator scheduling.

Run a Scheduling Comparison

It's very hard to provide explicit "if-A-then-B" strategies for *SimTower's* elevator controls. In a shifting, variable simulation environment such as this, it's just not possible to accurately compare scheduling options. But if you're like me and you can't help but explore settings and monkey around with controls, you might want to set up the following test.

Open up a good-sized tower, if you have one saved. (If not, then use the Kickstart feature—see the Kickstart section at the end of Chapter 1—and quickly build a 15-story building.) Look for a 15-floor section running from lobby to lobby, preferably one in which each floor is homogeneous all the way across—that is, individual floors are either all-Office, all-Fast Food, all-Condo, or all-whatever. The idea is to have floors that are balanced, population-wise, from one end to the other.

Now, place two Standard elevator shafts side-by-side in the middle of the section, both running from the first floor lobby up the 15th floor Sky Lobby. Give both the same number of cars—a full rack of eight, if you can afford it, but at least four. Finally, use your Bulldozer tool to destroy any other transportation in the section—Elevators, Stairs, or Escalators.

In this situation, each elevator shaft should receive roughly the same amount of traffic. Play with the controls on each. Watch how different types of scheduling compare by observing the passengers waiting for service by each shaft. Which shaft has the longer waiting lines? Which one has more stressed-out and red-faced passengers? Do "Express to Bottom" or "Express to Top" settings expedite traffic to any degree?

Figure 12-12. Head-to-Head Competition. Put two elevators side-by-side in the center of a busy tower, give them different scheduling settings . . . then watch and see who has more red-faced passengers during rush hour.

Figure 12-13. Destination Spot Check. Another way to gauge an elevator shaft's scheduling efficiency is to directly examine the Sims who use it. Open up a full elevator car during rush hour and click on each of its passengers. Where are they going? How stressed are they?

Waiting Floor Strategy

Lobby floors always generate the heaviest elevator traffic. In general, you should assign at least three waiting elevator cars to lobby floors at the bottom of a shaft. This keeps your elevator system ready for the onset of *SimTower's* various "rush" time periods.

However, after a rush hour gets in full swing, waiting floor assignments cease to make any difference, unless you have your Waiting Car Response number set high (which you shouldn't). Your cars will be all over the place, responding to service calls without any time to return to waiting floors.

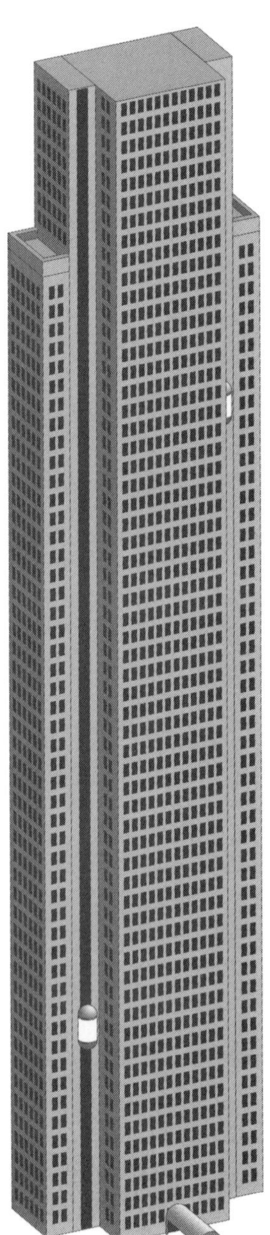

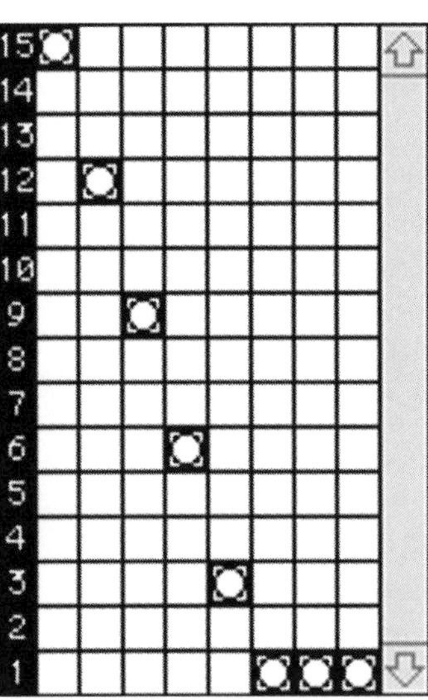

Figure 12-14. "Waiting" Scheme.
Cars belong where demand is heaviest. In this 15-floor-high Standard elevator shaft, the busy first floor lobby gets three waiting cars. The other five cars are spread evenly along the shaft.

Waiting floors actually become a bit more important when traffic is light. If you have cars spread throughout the shaft, Sims who summon elevators during off-hours don't have to wait long for a hoist. Your goal should be to produce a near-zero waiting period for elevator service during off-hours. If you can keep Sim stress levels low, then plenty of reserve remains for when peak hour traffic produces the inevitable elevator waiting lines.

F
1
B1
B2
PET
B7
B8

Part 4

Evaluation, Pricing, and Special Features

F
F
1
B1
B2
B7
B8
PET

13 Pricing and Evaluation

Money. We all need it. Real money is really nice, of course, but in lieu of that, virtual money can be satisfying. In *SimTower*, after you blow your first wad of cash, the money comes kind of slowly. It trickles in daily from Fast Food or, later, from Hotel income. When the quarterly rental income finally comes in—well, it's just not enough, is it?

How do you get more money?

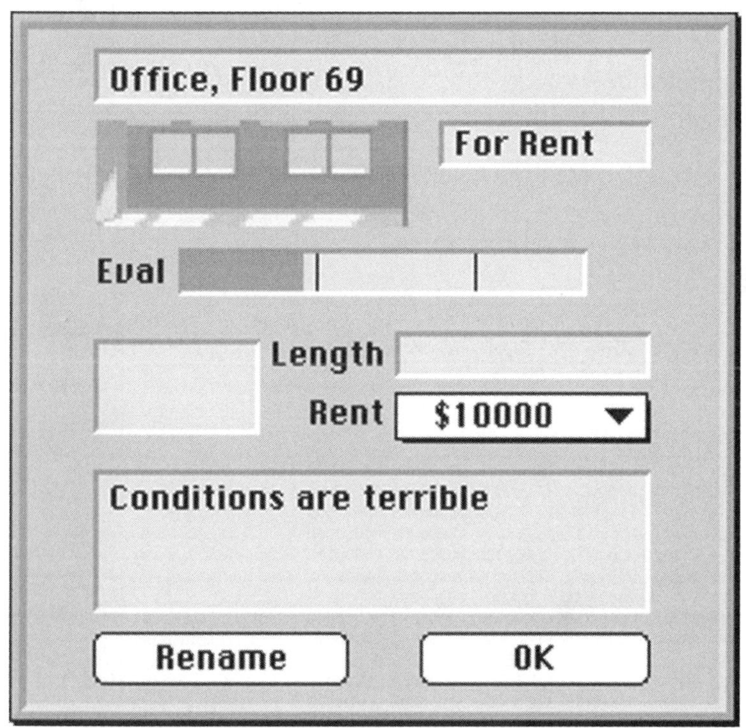

Figure 13-1. Unhappy Campers. Here's what you want to avoid. Regularly check your evaluations and adjust prices.

How to Collect Lots of SimMoney

Okay—one easy way is to boot *SimTower* late at night. Use the Kickstart cheat to double your opening bank account. Then, build up a tight, efficient little three-star tower with plenty of Security units. Leave the computer on. Go to bed. (You do have a screen-

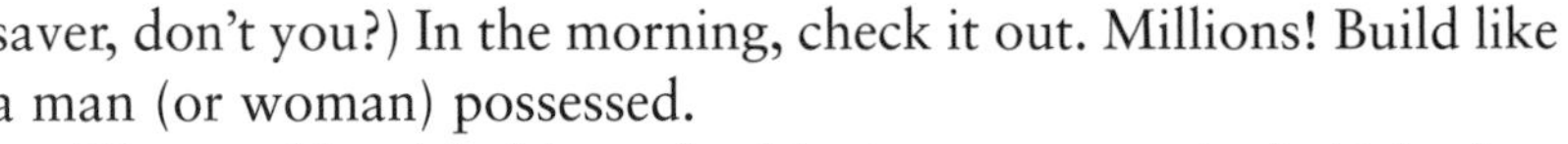

saver, don't you?) In the morning, check it out. Millions! Build like a man (or woman) possessed.

The trouble with this method is that you can miss half the fun. Terrorist bombers, fires, and VIPs in your Hotel may come and go, leaving behind nary a trace of such a major event.

An even easier (and more insidious) way to get mega-money comes courtesy of Mark Kupferman of New Haven, Connecticut, via the Maxis *SimTower* folder on America Online. It's a beauty, but it virtually eliminates many of the strategic elements of the game.

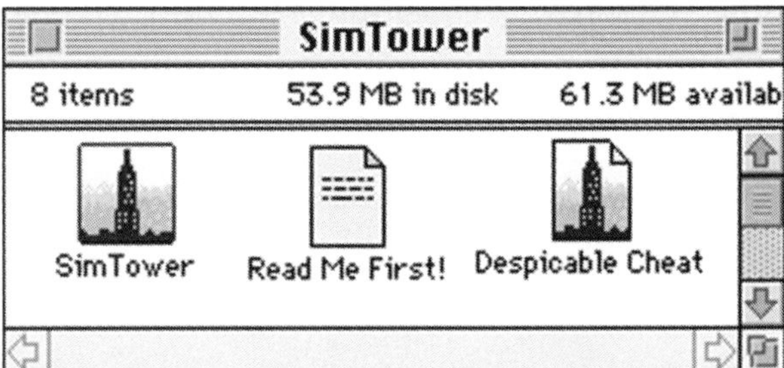

Figure 13-2.
For Hex Maniacs Only. To cheat your way to a fat wad of cash, create a New Tower file, name it something appropriate (right), then close the file. Reopen it with a good disk editor (like Norton Disk Editor, used here) and mess with the code. In this instance (below), I highlighted the file's fifth byte, then changed it from 00 to 05. To see my result, check out Figure 13-3.

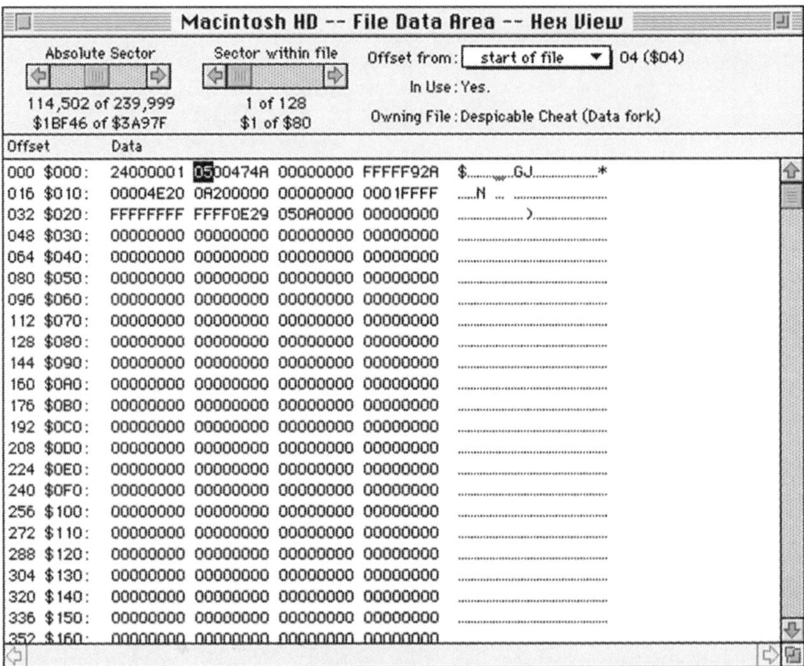

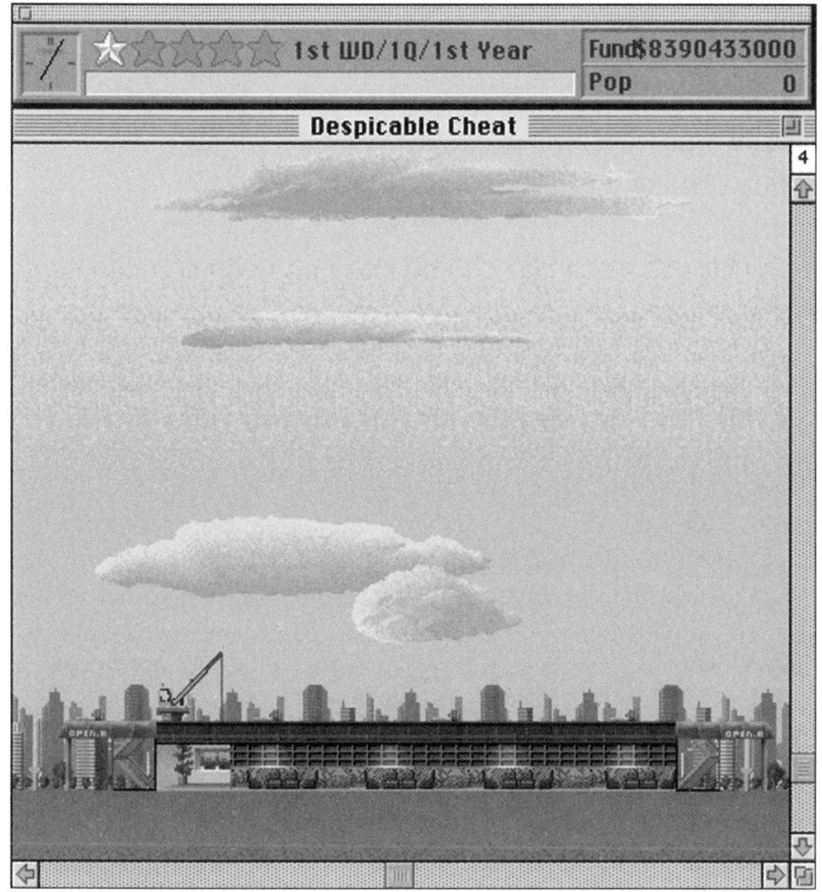

Figure 13-3. Despicable Fund. Yeah, I cheated. I don't feel good about it, either. Maybe an $8.4 billion head start is a bit much.

Here's Mr. Kupferman's money-grubbing strategy to get virtually unlimited *SimTower* funds:

1. Create a new tower—just a section or two of lobby is enough—then save it.
2. Name the file "Despicable Cheat" (or whatever you want, but I believe it's always best to be honest).
3. Quit the *SimTower* application.
4. Re-open "Despicable Cheat" using a disk editor application such as Norton Disk Editor.
5. Now, go to the fifth byte of the file. (In Norton Disk Editor, just press the right arrow key four times. See Figure 13-2.) It should be "00."

6. Change the fifth byte to any number. (Kupferman suggests "55.")
7. Write the sector to disk (or save the file, depending on what software you are using), then quit the disk editor.
8. Reopen the file with the *SimTower* application.

According to Mr. Kupferman, "You should now have approximately $559,000,000 to play with, and the program never knows what happened."

When I tried this trick using Norton Disk Editor, I ended up with far, far more than $559 million. In fact, I had so many billions of dollars that the number overlapped the Fund label on my Info Bar! So I reopened the file with Norton Disk Editor and changed the fifth byte to "05" instead of "55." When I again opened "Despicable Cheat" in *SimTower*, I still had quite a chunk of change in my Fund (see Figure 13-3).

Fine. But maybe you want a challenge. Maybe you want to play *SimTower* the way it's supposed to be played. The idea is to nurture and develop a tower, to make the right pricing decisions based on evaluation—in other words, to keep in constant touch with your tenants.

Basics of Pricing and Evaluation

In *SimTower*, pricing strategy and evaluation strategy are so intertwined that it's nearly impossible to discuss one without making reference to the other. But before we get into strategy talk, let's quickly (and I mean quickly) review the mechanics of how each works.

Pricing: How It Works

Adjusting prices couldn't be easier. When you build a rental property, its quarterly rent is set at a default rate—$10,000 for Offices, $15,000 for Shops.

To change a property's rent:

1. Click the Magnifying Glass on the property to open its Facility Window.
2 Click and hold on Rent.

3. Drag the highlight to the desired rental rate. There are four—High, Average (the default rate), Low, and Very Low.
4. Release the mouse button.
5. Click OK.

Figure 13-5. Pricing Map. Here's an overall look at the rental rates in your building. Scan the blue (Very Low) properties from time to time to see if you can raise rates without lowering evaluations.

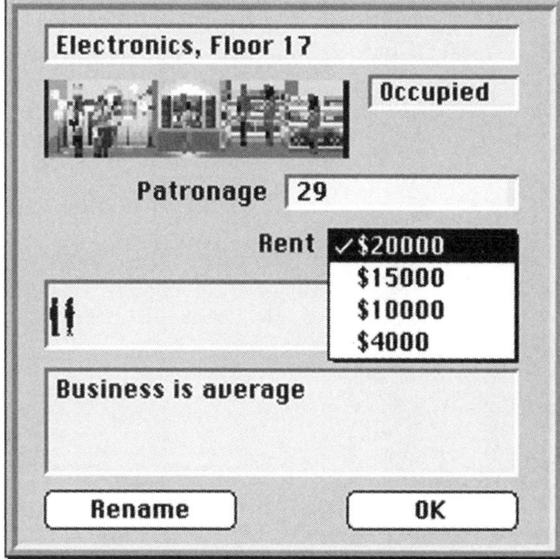

Figure 13-4. How to Adjust Pricing. Open the Facility Window. Click on Rent (or Price if it's a Condo), drag the highlight to the desired rental rate, then release.

Follow the same steps to adjust the sales price of a Condo. (The default price is $150,000.) But be quick. Once a Condo sells, there's no changing the price. And if a Condo is placed on a floor connected by transportation anytime between 7:00 A.M. and 9:00 P.M., it sells almost immediately.

You can get an overall look at your tower's pricing structure by clicking on the Pricing button in the Map Window. When you do this, the properties in both the Map and Edit Windows become color-coded according to the four pricing rates—High (red), Average (yellow), Low (green), and Very Low (blue). Use the Map Window to scroll quickly to particular areas, then click on individid-

ual properties in the Edit Window to compare the price level with the current evaluation. Scan the blue (Very Low) properties in particular to see if you can raise rates without lowering evaluations.

Here's one other very important pricing fact to remember. Properties with rents set to the lowest of the four pricing levels *never* generate a Terrible (red) evaluation. This becomes important in massive towers. For more on this, see the section on massive towers later in this chapter.

Evaluation: How It Works

SimTower's evaluation mode reveals how your tenants feel about your tower and its management (you). There are three levels of evaluation—Excellent (blue), Good (yellow), and Terrible (red). To check any property's evaluation, simply click on the property in the Edit Window to open its Facility Window.

Figure 13-6. Office Evaluation.
Open the Facility Window and check the color of the Eval bar. If the tenant has expressed a specific problem, it will be listed in the message box at the bottom.

Figure 13-7. Shop Evaluation.
Open the Facility Window and check the color of the Patronage bar. If it's red and the shop's more than a few days old, you might want to lower the rent.

You can get an overall look at your tenant evaluations by clicking on the Eval button in the Map Window. When you do this, the properties in both the Map and Edit Windows become color-coded according to the three evaluation levels. Use the Map Window to scroll quickly to red problem areas, then click on individual properties in the Edit Window to check for more specific information or to make pricing changes.

Remember that office evaluations are based on average worker stress, while food or retail store evaluations are based on amount of traffic. This distinction is discussed in depth later in this chapter.

Figure 13-8. Evaluation Map. Here's an overall look at the tenant evaluations in your building. Examine red (Terrible) properties and see if there are specific complaints about transportation. If not, try lowering rents.

General Strategies

Different-sized towers require different pricing and evaluation strategies to maintain good growth. Young towers are hungry for that basic nutrient, cash. Mature towers gobble cash, too, but also need a significant population influx—a consideration that can sometimes supersede your desire to maximize cash. Massive towers generate plenty of revenue, but *SimTower's* transportation limits can push tenant stress to the breaking point. When that happens, you have to get really serious about persuasion.

Young Tower: Focus on Income

In the early stages of your tower's life (up to population 5,000 or so—that is, one-, two-, and three-star towers), your most pressing need is cash for further development. Thus, your focus should be on maximizing income. Spend lots of time in Evaluation mode, pushing up rents as high as you can without suffering Terrible (red) ratings. It's a bit time-consuming and tedious, but you'll build up a good-sized war chest.

The 5 A.M. Rule (All Offices and Shops)

Crafty *SimTower* landlords know that Sim tenants are amazingly gullible renters. Tenants are happiest when rents are low, of course. But Sims pay whatever rent you have designated at payment time, regardless of when you raised or lowered the rent.

In other words, you can keep the rent level artificially low all quarter, then suddenly raise it just before collection time for the next quarter. (In *SimTower*, all Offices and Shops pay their rent promptly at 5:00 A.M. on the first weekday (1st WD) of each quarter.)

Figure 13-9.
What a Scrooge Job.
The magic hour approaches. At 5:00 A.M. on the first business workday (1st WD) of the quarter, Offices and Shops pay their rent. To maximize rental income, pause the game just before 5:00 A.M. . . .

Figure 13-10.
. . . then click on Office/Shop tenants, and raise their rent. Continue the game. After the 5:00 A.M. rent collection, you might want to lower rents again to maintain good evaluations through the next quarter.

Of course, as your tower gets bigger, this becomes not only unscrupulous, but also ludicrously time-consuming and tedious. When you have hundreds of rental properties, it can take hours (depending on machine speed and patience) to click on each individual renter, jack up the rent, then, after the 5:00 A.M. collection, click on everybody again and lower the rents.

Mature Tower: Focus on Population

When you reach four- and five-star ratings, a healthy income remains important. But by now, your tower is packed full of rental properties and quarterly manipulation of Office and Shop rents to maximize money can take you hours and can be stunningly boring. So, forget money for awhile. Focus instead on increasing your tower traffic—after all, it's a considerable jump from 5,000 to 10,000 inhabitants, the population milestone for the five-star rating.

Figure 13-11. Four-Star. Once you reach this rating, focus on increasing population rather than maximizing money. To do this . . .

Figure 13-12. . . . select the Eval button in the Map Window. Then, scan the building, lowering rents as far as necessary to achieve blue (Excellent) evaluations.

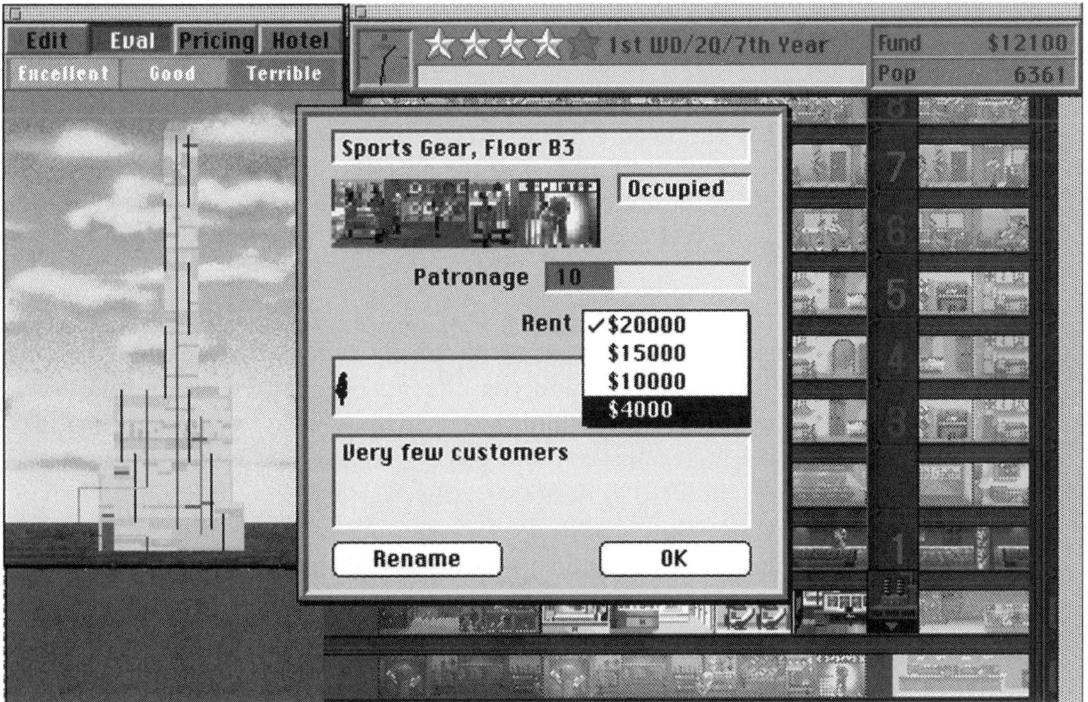

A good way to keep your population growing is to scan through your building, lowering rents. This way, even rainy days won't endanger your tenancy rates, and all those satisfied blue folks continue to pull new Sims into the building. Be smart, though—don't lower rents in bustling areas. Offer relief only to struggling tenants, but when you do, make sure to drop the rent far enough to make a difference in the evaluation rating. In many (if not most) cases, this requires reducing the rent to the very lowest of the four possible rates.

Massive Tower: Focus on Survival

If you've got the RAM, you can build some really serious towers. Huge, monstrous things, packed full of activity. The problem is, you've got limited transportation for all those people. *SimTower* restricts the number of elevator shafts (24) and the number of stairs/escalators (64 total).

Of course, it's very important to wisely place your transportation devices. (For more on this, see Chapter 12.) Yet even the most perfectly designed transit system becomes strained by the traffic in a gigantic tower. Thus, you'll have to resort to a tried-and-true method of keeping people happy—bribery.

Open all red-evaluated properties and lower their rents to the cheapest rate. Do the same every time you add a new property. What the heck, you don't need the money, right? In a massive tower you can hardly spend it fast enough, even if every property has Very Low rent. The goal now is to keep tenants. You want them to be happy. You want to click on the Eval button and see a contented blue monument to your magnanimity.

Daily Versus Quarterly Income

Shops and Offices pay rent quarterly. Other types of properties bring you daily returns—Fast Food, Restaurants, Cinema, Party Halls, and Hotel rooms. In general, it's nice to have both kinds of income. Daily income lets you respond quickly to situations—another car in a suddenly overworked elevator shaft, for example. Quarterly income then provides the big dollars for serious expansion and/or remodeling efforts.

Figure 13-13.
How Low Can You Get?
When transportation systems are pushed to the limit in a really massive tower, bribe your Lilliputians by lowering rents to the lowest rate. If you do, they won't leave—no matter how bad conditions get.

Here's a comparative look at the income generated by all types of tenants. It's important to note that these figures are based on Average rental rates and Good business traffic—two variables on which you cannot always count.

Daily/Quarterly Income (By Tenant)			
Tenant	**Daily Income**	**Quarterly Income**	**Construction Cost**
Party Hall	$20,000	$60,000	$100,000
Movie Theater	$15,000	$45,000	$500,000
Restaurant	$6,000	$18,000	$200,000
Hotel Suite	$6,000	$18,000	$100,000
Shop	—	$15,000	$100,000
Office	—	$10,000	$40,000
Fast Food	$3,000	$9,000	$100,000
Twin Hotel	$3,000	$9,000	$50,000
Single Hotel	$2,000	$6,000	$20,000

Raw numbers like those in the table above are interesting, but fail to tell the whole story. For example, Party Halls look like the deal of the century. They have a greater payout than Movie Theaters, yet cost far less to build with none of the costly upkeep. (Changing movies each year for $300,000 is a killer expense, isn't it?) But remember, Movie Theaters pull in outside customers and significantly increase commercial traffic.

Another example: Restaurants offer the same rate of return as Hotel Suites. But veteran *SimTower* builders know that Restaurants are notoriously hard to keep at the blue evaluation level ("Business is Good"), cost twice as much to build as Suites, and are adversely affected by rain. Hotel Suites, on the other hand, are occupied daily (as long as your Housekeeping staff keeps them clean), require only periodic evaluation checks, and their rent can often be boosted to a High rate of $9,000 per day for several days in a row.

One last example: Offices are much cheaper to build than Shops, yet over time, they bring in roughly the same amount of income. In terms of cash flow, then, Offices are often a better investment. However, Shops bring far more people into your tower than do Offices. Thus, if you're trying to reach a population milestone in order to graduate to the next star rating, you might want to focus on developing your tower shopping areas first.

Stress: How It Affects Evaluation and Pricing

Property evaluations can be confusing. Sometimes, tenants get fed up in ways that seem illogical. Tucked in the middle of a row of happy blue Offices lurks that odd, cranky red one, disgusted with your management style. It's particularly frustrating when everything—rent, access to transportation—is exactly the same for the complainer as it is for the happy clams, and no reason for the bad evaluation appears in the message bar. So what's wrong? It seems illogical. It seems like *SimTower* simply scanned its supply of tenants and randomly selected one to be angry.

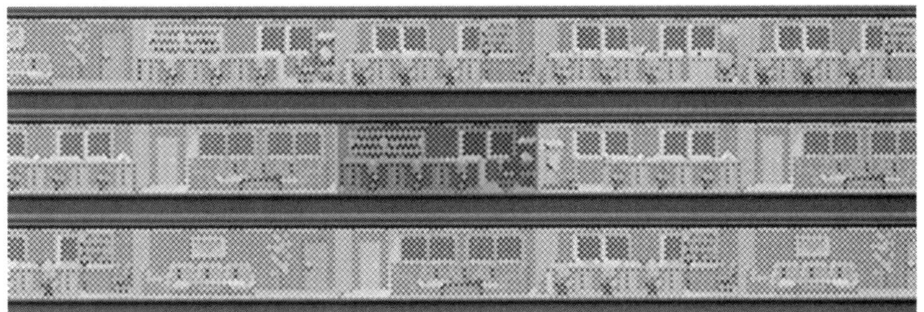

Figure 13-14. Prima Donna? What's wrong with the red tenant? Its rent and transportation access are the same as its contented blue neighbors.

But in fact, it's not illogical or random. To understand *SimTower's* property evaluations, you have to understand how they are derived from the stress levels of individual Sims.

Stress and Evaluation

Sims have pretty strong opinions about the conditions in the Offices where they work, the Shops where they shop, or the Hotel rooms where they stay. When you open the Tenant Window for any Sim, the Eval bar (see Figure 13-15) conveys that opinion in living color. If the Sim happens to be from "Outside," then the Eval bar refers to his/her destination in the tower.

This Eval bar uses the same color coding as Facility Window evaluations—blue ("I'm happy!"), yellow ("I'm okay!"), and red ("I'm fed up!"). What affects the Eval bar? The answer: Stress. But what causes stress in individual Sims? Again, the answer in a word: Waiting. Sims *hate* to wait. And if their rent is high, they *really* hate to wait.

Only one thing forces Sims to wait, and that's your tower transportation system.

Figure 13-15. Stress. The Stress bar in this Tenant Window registers the Sim's stress during the current trip. The Eval bar registers his overall feelings about his place of origin or, if he's from Outside, his tower destination.

How SimTower Measures Stress

As your *SimTower* User's Manual explains, stress is calculated by the time (measured in number of frames) that it takes a Sim to make a trip to a tower destination. The longer it takes, the more stress builds up. The Stress bar in each Sim's Tenant Window registers the amount of stress generated by the current trip in the same blue-yellow-red color code. (Again, see Figure 13-15.) No stress rating appears when the Sim is not traveling.

When a Sim completes his trip, his final stress rating affects his Eval bar rating—again, the evaluation of his place of origin (if he lives or works in the building) or the evaluation of his tower destination (if he came from Outside).

How Stress Affects Office Evaluations

Still wondering how you get that one red complainer amidst a sea of blue Office evaluations? Remember, the overall evaluation of an Office is comprised of the average of all the Eval bar levels of its Office workers. And, as you've just seen, stressful trips bring down the Eval bar levels of individual Sims.

Figure 13-16. Elevator Haters. Some of these waiting folks are getting pretty red-faced (though in black and white, no one can see you scream). If several of the angry ones happen to be from the same Office, its overall evaluation can drop quickly.

Now, consider this. In a big tower, even the most perfectly-planned transit system can leave groups of Sims waiting at an elevator, burning red with anger. If several members of a waiting group happen to be from the same Office (not an uncommon occurrence) and your elevator leaves them waiting long enough, then all of their individual Eval bars begin to drop. This, in turn, lowers the average of their combined evaluations—that is, it lowers the Eval bar in the Office's Facility Window. Suddenly, you've got a Terrible Office, even though all of its neighbors are apparently happy.

Whatever the cause of a red Office evaluation, you'd better do something about it soon. Because once an Office posts a Terrible evaluation, it can be all downhill from there unless you put a stop to it.

How do you do that? Analyze your transportation grid in failed areas and try to improve it. Unfortunately, sometimes there's nothing you can do about transportation—you've got no money, or no more transportation devices are available. If that's the case, you have only one other option: Lower the rent.

How Price Affects Evaluation Levels

The overall evaluation level of any price-adjustable property—Office, Shop, Condo, or Hotel—can be directly manipulated by an increase or decrease of the pricing. Experiment with the High, Average, and Low pricing rates for a particular property. You'll see that the less you charge a tenant, the more you reduce the overall stress indicated by the Eval bar in the Facility Window.

Think of each Eval bar as representing 300 points. In general, High pricing decreases the overall evaluation by 30 points. Low pricing increases it by 30 points. Average pricing doesn't affect the evaluation either way.

Note that with Very Low pricing, a property's stress level becomes irrelevant. Sims put up with anything if the price is rock bottom. This becomes very important when massive towers push your transportation grid beyond its capacity. By lowering rents to their cheapest rate, you can ensure that tenants *never* leave!

The Word-of-Mouth System

Sims are simple folks, like you and me. (Well, okay—*you're* deep and complex. But I'm not.) They know what they like. And when they

find it, they spread the news. It is this *SimTower* "word-of-mouth" system that keeps your building bustling and healthy. Or not.

Here's how it works. In general, when a Sim arrives at a destination in your tower, he is deeply affected by its ambiance. Regardless of his personal level of stress, he bases his entire takeaway impression of the property on its evaluation as measured in its Facility Window—that is, the property's Eval or Patronage bar color.

Figure 13-17.
Loyal Customers.
Here's a store that clearly does things right. The Good evaluation means each of those five customers will return to the Clothes Barn tomorrow with a friend in tow.

If the place is rated Excellent (blue) he returns the next day that the place is open for business—and he brings a friend. If it is rated Good (yellow) he returns the next day, but alone. If it is rated Terrible (red) he boycotts the place.

This basic rule can be affected by other variables—for example, traffic reductions due to rainy days or sudden strains on your transit system caused by new construction. If a happy customer returns with an eager friend, but neither one of them can get to the store before boiling over with stress due to elevator congestion, well . . . both will gladly bail out of your tower to go check out that new California-style strip mall on the far side of town.

Overall, though, the "word-of-mouth" rule is strict and consistent. It works in the same manner for all Offices and Hotel rooms, and for all *established* Shops, Fast Food joints, and Restaurants.

Note the emphasis on the word "established" in the previous sentence. In some *SimTower* situations, an interesting modification of the "word-of-mouth" rule applies to newly-built commercial tenants.

New Commercial Tenants

It's not easy to start a business these days. In *SimTower*, no Shop, Fast Food joint, or Restaurant has more (or less) than 10 customers on its first day of operation. Unless rent is Very Low, a patronage of 10 is always considered "very few customers" for any commercial tenant, and thus, always results in a Terrible (red) rating.

Not to worry, though. Sims are willing to give a new place the benefit of the doubt. For new commercial tenants, the "word-of-mouth" rule is modified by a "customer stress level" corollary.

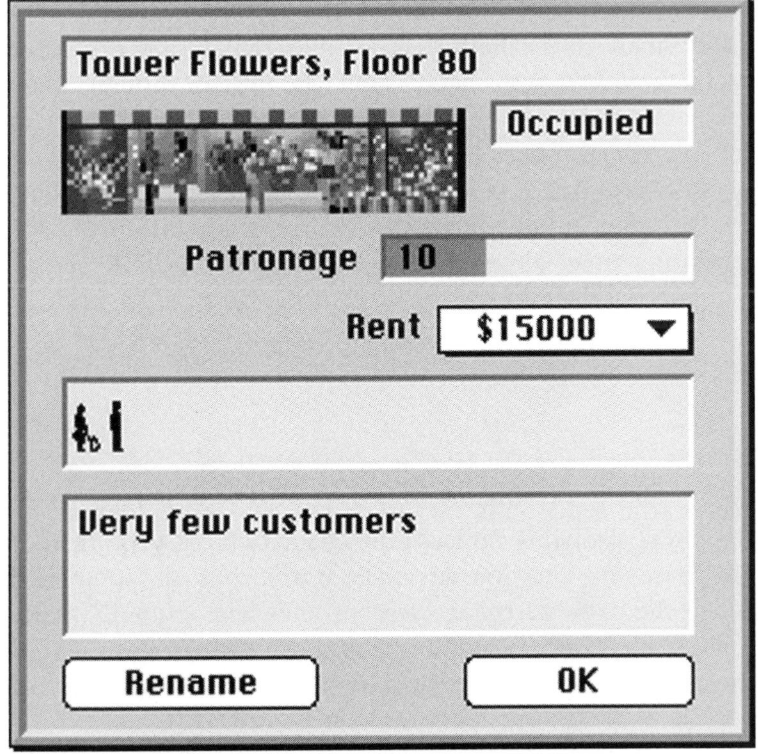

Figure 13-18.
Is the Flower Shop Failing?
No, it's just new. Each of those first 10 patrons who get there without much stress will bring back a friend tomorrow.

In this corollary, each of the 10 customers who visit a new Shop, Fast Food joint, or Restaurant on its first day bases his "word-of-mouth" opinion of the place on his own personal stress level. If the

customer doesn't encounter much waiting in his journey to a Shop and arrives with a healthy blue Stress bar in his Tenant Window, he returns the next day with a friend.

Note that in this case, "Good" stress isn't good enough for the survival of the Shop. If each of the 10 customers arrives with a Good (yellow) personal stress level, each returns alone the next day—again, patronage of only 10 people means a Terrible (red) rating for the Shop. If this continues for long, the Shop fails, and the shopkeeper vacates the premises.

This differs greatly from your Hotel and Office tenants, who start out with Excellent (blue) evaluations and can survive just fine at the yellow evaluation level.

A Note About Daily Commercial Traffic

If you open the Facility Window of any retail shop or food place shortly after it opens for the day, the Patronage number is ridiculously small, the evaluation is Terrible (red), and the message box says, "Very few customers." Don't be misled, though. The business story of any commercial tenant unfolds hourly in *SimTower's* version of real time.

In other words, customers trickle in throughout the day, and the Patronage number grows at a fairly steady ratio from opening to closing time, although Fast Food joints naturally see a huge bump in business during the lunch hour. Generally speaking, both the number of customers and the evaluation level increase every hour throughout the day.

How Pricing Affects Retail Shop Evaluations

As you've probably noticed, the evaluations of your retail shops are based not only on customer traffic, but also on rent level. When the day's patronage reaches anywhere from 15 to 24 customers, for example, a Shop tenant can give you any one of the three evaluations—red, yellow, or blue—depending on what rent you choose to charge him.

The chart on the following page shows how rent affects Shop evaluation at different patronage levels.

Retail Shop Evaluation Chart

Evaluation Color Code: Blue = Excellent
Yellow = Good
Red = Terrible

	Pricing Level			
	High	Average	Low	Very Low
0-7 customers/day	Red	Red	Red	Red
8-12	Red	Red	Red	Yellow
13-14	Red	Red	Red	Blue
15-19	Red	Red	Yellow	Blue
20-24	Red	Yellow	Blue	Blue
25-29	Yellow	Blue	Blue	Blue
30-above	Blue	Blue	Blue	Blue

When to Place Offices and Shops

When you place an Office or Shop, you collect the first rent when the tenant occupies the facility. After that, you collect rent at 5:00 A.M. on the first workday (1st WD) of each new quarter. So, you might think that by placing Offices and Shops on the weekend (WE), you can double the first round of rent—that is, collect rent when the property is first occupied, then collect again within 24 hours when the new quarter begins.

In fact, this is true with your shop tenants. However, keep in mind that *SimTower* appraises its Shops at the end of each quarter. Since Shops never have more than 10 customers on the first day of business, no Shop that opens on a weekend can build enough traffic to get a good appraisal for that quarter.

Don't wait too long to build Offices, either. Offices built after 1:00 P.M. remain closed until the morning of the next workday. As mentioned in Chapter 6, all Offices are closed on Weekends, so if you place an Office after 1:00 P.M. on the second workday (2nd WD) of the current quarter, you don't get a renter (or rent) until the new quarter begins.

TIP On the first workday (1st WD), develop shopping areas first. Then build Offices—but finish them before 1:00 P.M. on the second work day (2nd WD), or you miss the rent deadline for the current quarter and they sit empty all weekend.

1
B1
B2
B7
B8

14 Special Events and Features

Okay, your traffic flows smoothly. Your elevators are brilliantly regulated. Your shops burst with business. Your residents are happy as clams. The phone rings. Some guy says hello. He mentions a bomb.

Or maybe fire breaks out on Floor 42, miles from your nearest Security team.

Or maybe it just rains like hell.

SimTower, like all good simulations, keeps you on your toes with special events such as these. How should you respond? Sometimes, prompt action can save the day. Other times, only preventive measures already taken can prevent catastrophe. And in some cases, there is absolutely nothing you can do but try to weather the storm.

Rain

Rain falls approximately every five days in *SimTower*. Wet commuter conditions have no effect, of course, on the Condo and Hotel people who reside in your tower. Nor does rain deter your

Figure 14-1.
Rain, Rain, Go Away.
Who cares about thirsty grass and trees and stuff? You're disrupting urban commerce!

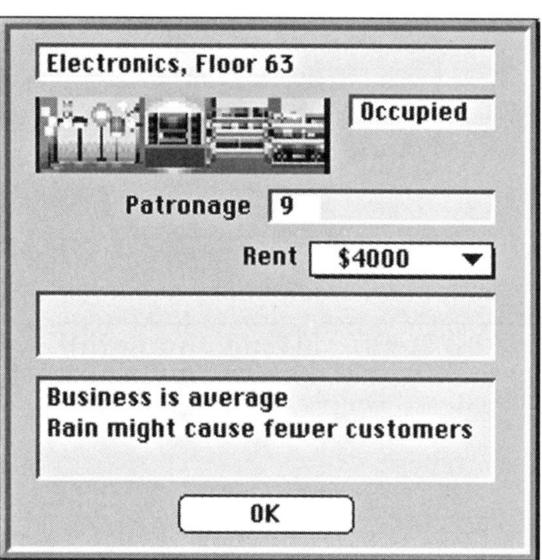

Figure 14-2.
Rain cuts business from "outside" customers by a solid 20 to 30 percent in your shops and food outlets. But a good-sized office and resident population can provide enough traffic to keep your commercial tenants out of the red.

hardy workers (Office, Fast Food, Hotel staff) from filling up your building each day.

However, many "outside" patrons of your tower's commercial zone are wimps who don't like getting wet. In fact, rainy days cut your outside traffic anywhere from 20 to 30 percent.

Unfortunately, there's not much you can do to pull in outside traffic on a rainy day. Fortunately, well-developed office and residential areas can provide enough customers to keep your commercial areas healthy in a downpour. The key is to strike a balance from the very beginning. Focus equal attention on office, residential, and commercial development as you build your tower. It pays off in the long run.

Bomb Threats

Terrorists. I hate these guys. Fortunately, the weasels strike only once every five years, and they focus their sick intent on towers with ratings of two, three, or four stars. They phone in the morning with their nasty threats. Then, your security forces have until 3:00 P.M. to find the bomb, unless you choose to pay the blackmail fee of $300,000.

Well-placed Security units can usually find a bomb and defuse it before anything bad happens. If they do, the whole event costs you nothing. Decide quickly, though. If you wait too long after the phone threat appears (see Figure 14-3), the *SimTower* program automatically pays the terrorist if you have sufficient funds.

Blackmail from Terrorists!
They demand $300000 or a hidden bomb will explode at 3 O'clock.
Pay Them
Find the Bomb

Figure 14-3. Hello?
Hey, it's the local bomb guy. What should you do? If you've got no cash, you've got no choice.

SimTower terrorists place a bomb randomly in the tower. In response, your guards follow a strict procedure: From each Security post, six guards fan out to adjacent floors, one guard per floor. One searches his home floor, three go in one direction (up or down); two go in the opposite direction. All search teams start at the far right of the building, then sweep across to the left. When each guard completes his floor sweep, he moves up or down to the next unexplored floor and starts a new right-to-left sweep.

Given this procedure, you can see how important the strategic placement of Security offices can be. If two Security units are based on the same floor or within three floors of each other, guards from both units overlap and search the same floor together—a

Security forces from your Security Offices are on their way to find the bomb. Good luck...
Hurry!

Figure 14-4. Job Security.
If you don't give in to blackmail, your Security forces fan out in search of the bomb. Whatever you pay these guys, it's not enough.

wasteful and potentially deadly duplication of resources. The best strategy is to space your Security facilities evenly throughout the tower (about every 11 floors, including underground levels).

Interestingly, it appears that *SimTower* terrorists use only bizarre "smart bombs." When a detonation occurs, the blast waves pass harmlessly through any nearby lobbies, elevators, stairs, escalators, Security or Housekeeping units, Recycling Centers, the Metro Station, and the Cathedral—in other words, any transportation device or any facility that can't be bulldozed.

Security was not able to find the bomb in time! The bomb has exploded on floor 57!
Oh No!
60
60
57
55
54

Figure 14-5. Bomb Aftermath. Next time, get more Security beforehand.

Fire

Fires can occur in towers rated at three or more stars. Horrific towering infernos are no fun. As with bomb threats, you get the option to pay your way out of disaster—in this case, $500,000 to a helicopter fire crew (see Figure 14-6) with pinpoint hose accuracy. If you don't have the cash, you have to rely on your Security forces to extinguish the blaze.

Regardless of your choice, the fire always begins in the morning and won't be finally quenched until 9:00 that night. In the meantime, the tower evacuates, so you lose an entire day's worth of business.

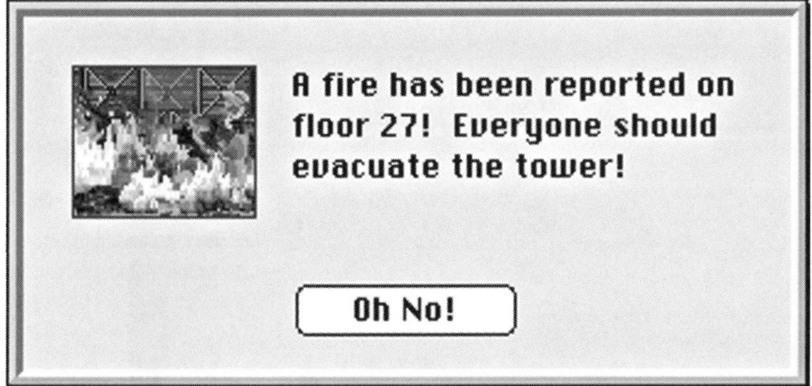

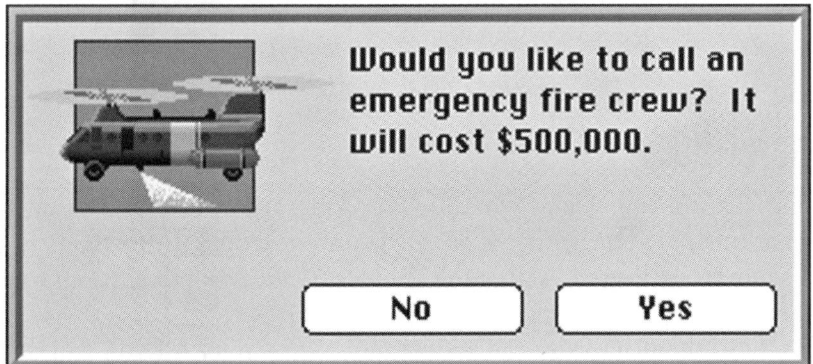

Figure 14-6. Fire Crew. Fires don't hurt anybody, but they can be brutal to your bank account. If you happen to have half a million bucks just lying around, it's best to hire a helicopter crew.

If you've been fastidious about placing Security offices every 10 or 11 floors, it may be cheaper to fight the fire yourself. Then again, it may not. Consider that the loss of only five retail shops (at a cost of $100,000 apiece to rebuild) equals the payout to a helicopter

fire crew. Unless contained immediately, fires can cause millions of dollars in damage, not to mention the cost of lost business.

On the other hand, it's not easy to keep half a million dollars stashed in your fund. Just remember that if you survive your first fire, you don't see another one for at least seven years.

Figure 14-7. Fire Up, Team! And quickly, or we'll all be toast in the morning.

Hotel Bugs

Bugs are not evil. That's what I tell my kids, anyway. You just don't want them in your pantry, is all. Or your hotel room. Unfortunately, if your Housekeeping staff can't get to a *SimTower* Hotel room for three straight days, cockroaches come in droves.

Once bugs happen, the room is unsalvageable. All you can do is bulldoze it. And you'd better do it fast. Bugs spread horizontally from an infested Hotel room, traveling one room in each direction per day. Fortunately, a bug infestation does not spread vertically to other floors, nor does it extend to properties other than Hotel rooms.

Figure 14-8.
Three Days of the Cockroach.
If a short-handed Housekeeping staff can't reach a room for three days in a row, this is what happens.

Figure 14-9. Bug Row.
Here, you can see how an infestation spreads horizontally room-by-room, but not vertically. Bugs from a dirty room on Floor 20 eventually cover the whole length of the floor, but leave hotel rooms above and retail shops below untouched.

VIP Visit

A VIP only visits a tower that has achieved a three-star rating. As you know, "VIP" stands for Very Irritating and Pompous, particularly if you don't cater to the guy in a big way. Don't be proud. Remember, one bad word from Limo Boy can stunt your tower's progress.

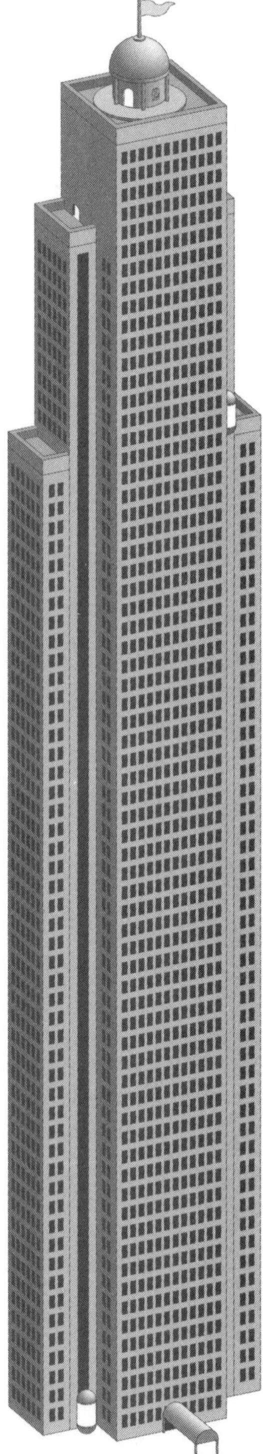

You are notified early in the day when the VIP makes his reservations. You also learn on which floor he wishes to stay. (See Figure 14-10.) Just to be safe, go to that floor and find all the Hotel Suites there. Drop their rates clear down to $1,500, the lowest level.

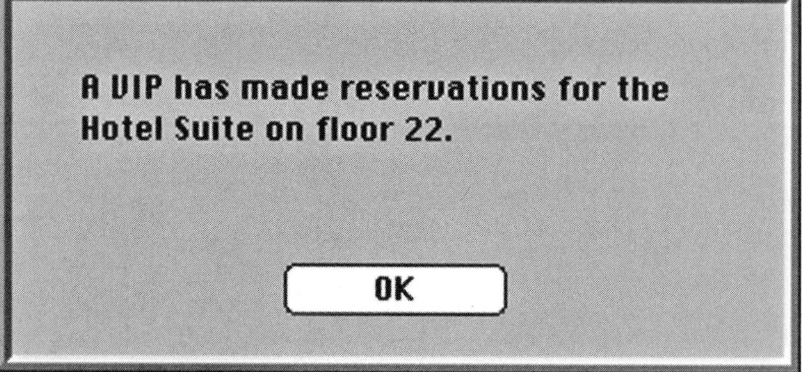

A VIP has made reservations for the
Hotel Suite on floor 22.
OK

Figure 14-10. VIP Reservation.
He's coming! Get to Floor 22 and drop all Suite room rates to $1,500.

Figure 14-11. VIP Arrival.
He's here! Quickly, figure out how to grease the elevators for his trip up to Floor 22 from your Parking Garage.

When the VIP arrives, you again receive notification of this event. For some reason, his limo drops him off in the Parking Garage. (Seems awfully clandestine, doesn't it?) A quick scan of transportation connected to your Parking levels may reveal the VIP himself—he's a bright yellow Sim, very ostentatious for such a little guy. Once you determine which elevator he's in, do what you can to expedite his trip. You might even want to deactivate elevator service in that shaft to all floors below the one on which his Hotel Suite is located. Once he's in his room, put multiple waiting cars on his floor. The less time he has to wait, the happier he is.

If the VIP's stay is a good one, you are informed of this, and your tower can now achieve a four-star rating—once you've reached all the other requisite milestones, of course. However, if the snooty fellow gives you the thumbs down, take heart. He returns every nine years until you get it right.

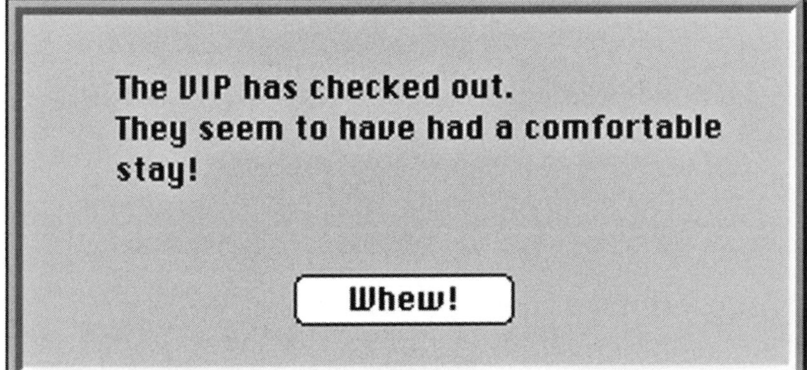

Figure 14-12. VIP Seal of Approval He's gone! Now you can graduate to a four-star rating and live happily ever after.

Buried Treasure

Ever wonder what a piece of eight really looks like? Ever had a hankering to fondle doubloons? Well, *SimTower's* the game for you, my friend. Because lurking down there in the dirt beneath your tower lies a chest of ancient buried pirate booty. You have to dig fairly early, though. Buried treasure can be found only at the one-star, two-star, or three-star rating level.

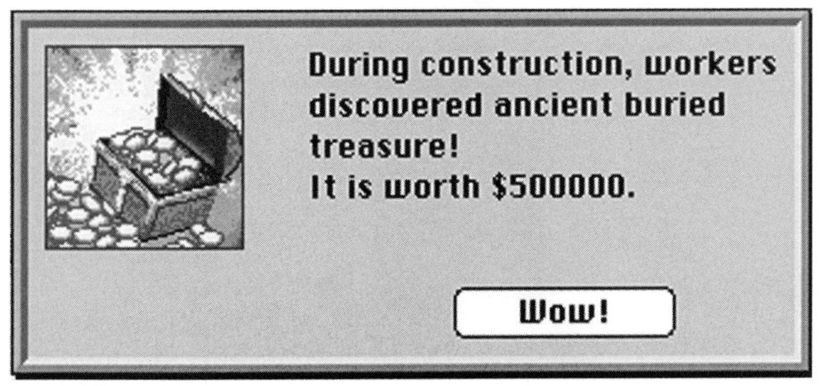

Figure 14-13. Motherlode. Aren't ancient pirates great? They always leave stuff like this laying around.

At the one-star rating, the only thing you can put underground is Fast Food shops. If you build a cluster of six shops with a dimension of 2 x 3, you find the treasure, worth $200,000. At the two- and three-star rating levels, you have to do a bit more rooting around the basement, but the treasure is then worth $500,000.

Santa

Yes, the jolly Red Elf himself—and his sleigh, reindeer, the whole nine yards. What kind of dreary SimWorld would it be without him? You'll hear the jingle bells at precisely 9:00 P.M. on the weekend (WE) of every year's fourth quarter (4Q). Click on the red dot that appears on the right side of the Map Window. Then watch your Edit Window. By midnight, show's over.

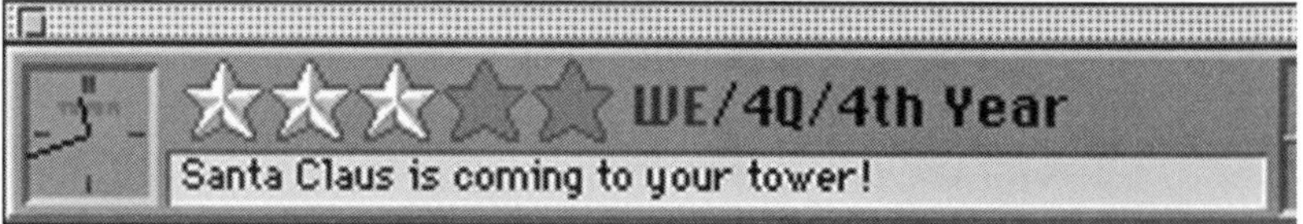

Figure 14-14. Do You Hear Bells? Ah, must be the end of another year. Check your Info Bar message window.

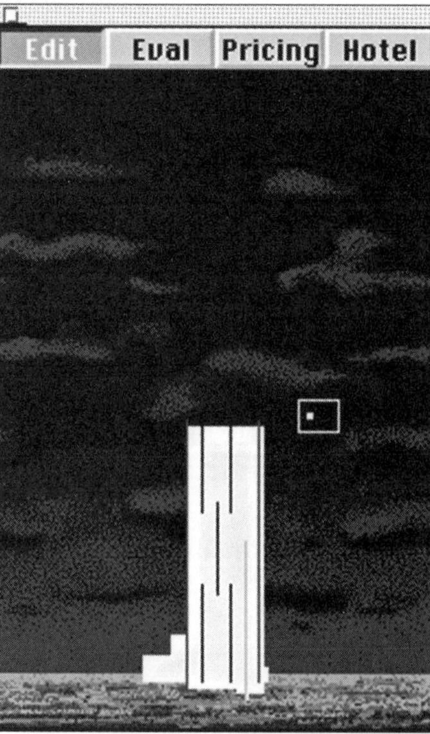

Figure 14-15. See that little red dot moving across your Map Window? Click on it . . .

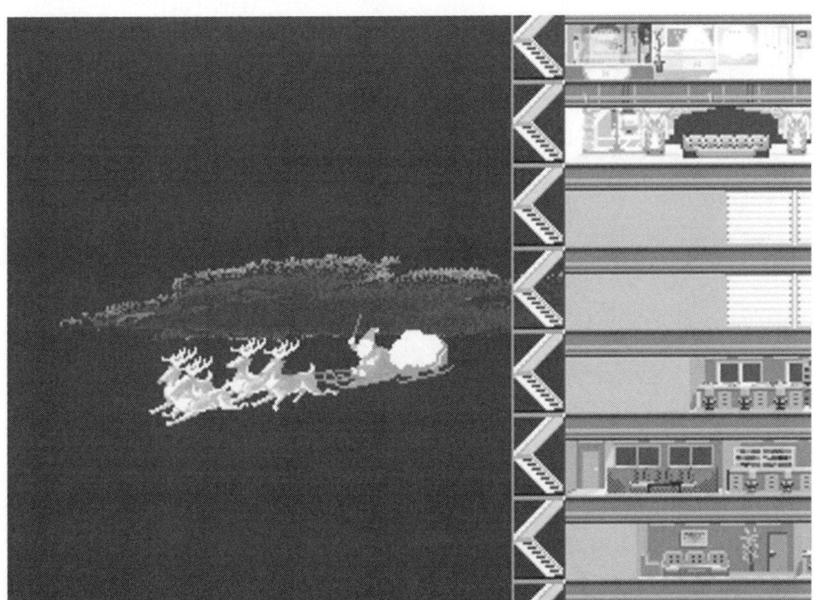

Figure 14-16.
. . . then check out the Edit Window. Ho ho ho!

The Tower Event

SimTower wouldn't let you take that final, glorious step from five-star status to a Tower rating without some kind of ceremony. It just wouldn't be right. So keep an eye on your Cathedral on the weekends after you achieve five-star status. Sorry, no screen shot here, and that's all I'm going to say about it. You'll just have to wait to see this one on your own.

F
F
1
B1
B2
PET
PET
B7
B8
PET

ST Interview with Yoot Saito, Creator of SimTower

The following interview is actually a cyber-conversation, conducted via the Internet. After all, Yoot Saito and I live quite a few thousand miles apart. And although Yoot is fluent in English, he felt more comfortable answering my questions in Japanese. So we worked out an elaborate and thoroughly 1990's sort of interview process.

I posted questions to Yoot's electronic mailbox (listed at the end of his Foreword to this book, by the way). In Tokyo, Yoot wrote answers in his native language and faxed them to Maxis representatives. Maxis faxed the answers to Brett Skogen, my project editor at Prima Publishing, who passed them on to Melinda McRae, our translator. Melinda translated Yoot's answers into English and E-mailed them to me. I edited the translated answers and E-mailed them back to Yoot. Yoot and I passed them back and forth a couple of times. When Yoot was satisfied that we had interpreted his responses accurately, I E-mailed the interview back to Prima for final editorial processing.

All of this global networking happened in the space of a few days—over a holiday weekend, no less.

Rick Barba: Tell us about your background, education, and other influences.

Yoot Saito: My major at University was architecture, but I think my personal vocation throughout life has always been "Innocent Questioner." Mr. Richard Saul Wurman, author of *Information Anxiety,* greatly influenced the development of my personal philosophy. The most important thing, always, is to ask questions and seek real knowledge. If one holds passion for knowledge, even with regard to the mundane, everyday things in life, then the world can be more fully understood and shown to others—in *SimTower* or other games, for instance. As a game designer, my role is the same as the kid in "Emperor's New Clothes."

Barba: So this personal philosophy makes you a better software designer?

Saito: I think so. I'm always curious about diverse things—life,

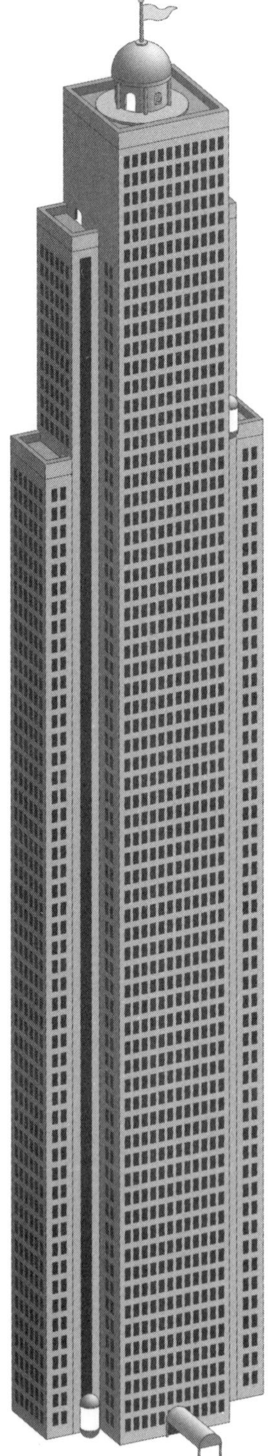

society, cultural systems, and the like—wanting to know the meaning of things. For example, when I work with the people at Maxis, I fly from Japan to San Francisco. I find myself questioning the mechanics of the airplane, how it flies, and I realize I don't know. We all take for granted that the plane will fly, and stop asking "how" and "why." We've stifled our natural human impulse to ask questions, to understand the underlying nature of things.

I start out my journey asking myself very complex, sophisticated questions, and my head (and Powerbook laptop) completely fills with ideas and new questions. It's part of my game design process. By the time I arrive at San Francisco airport, I haven't been able to sleep. (That's why I'm a zombie when I arrive at Maxis!) So my questions turn into those of a five-year-old child. But these childlike questions are often very fundamental, passionate ones—the ones too many of us begin to ignore as we grow older.

Today I looked through my office window at the convention center where a big aerospace show is being held. At lunchtime, I went over to look around, since I am very interested in this sort of event. Readers of this book are probably computer users who may be more interested in MacWorld or Windows Expo. Some people think that heavy industries or trade are not as innovative as the computer industry. But for me, the physical reality of a jet engine, the feeling of sitting in a helicopter seat, is much more deeply fascinating than some virtual reality moon-exploring system. In fact, the VR flight simulator systems looked really cheap next to a real helicopter—they provided no impact or real feeling. I think computer world designers focus too exclusively on the mechanical aspects of simulation. They need to be more sensitive to real-life, human feelings.

Barba: How did the idea for *SimTower* originate?

Saito: About three and a half years ago, when I was working on a simulation game called *Zaibatsu Bank,* I wanted to create a sort of theoretical model of traffic, using mathematical ordinals. Late one night, I was waiting in my building's lobby for an elevator, thinking about this traffic model. There are two cars in my building's shaft. I'd pushed the button, but instead of the closest car coming to my floor, the furthest car arrived first. This really irritated me! Of course, in my usual questioning way, I asked myself, "What happened here? How are these cars logically synchronized?" This was the beginning of *SimTower*.

Barba: Jeff Braun (co-founder, Chairman, and CEO of Maxis) says *SimTower* may be "the most genius thing we've ever developed" and describes you as "a rock-star groupie who now becomes a rock star himself." Is it true that your fascination with *SimCity* led you to meet with Will Wright? Can you tell us about that meeting?

Saito: Maxis' *SimCity* products share a unique quality, I think. For me, the original *SimCity,* in particular, was a very distinctive game. A friend at MIT introduced me to this strange piece of software a few years ago. He had a hard time putting *SimCity* into any sort of category. After playing it, I realized it's not just a game, but a thinking tool. That's what I like about Maxis. None of their products emphasize how fast you can move your finger on the controller to destroy things. Instead, they require you to *think*. Maxis makes products that are closest to what I imagine in my head.

I first met Will Wright in a hotel lobby at the MacWorld Expo. Chris Crawford, the designer of *Balance of Power,* was also there with us. We were discussing the details of a future meeting in Japan. I gave them my *Zaibatsu Bank* game, which is based on an economic system revolving around large companies such as the Mitsubishi cartel. I was honored to discover that Will thought it was a good logic model.

I met Will again at a panel discussion in Japan where we talked about various things. After that, Will and I spoke often on the telephone about my idea for *Tower* (the original name of the Japanese version of *SimTower*). Will was working on *SimCity 2000* then, and we'd discuss the different concepts and aims of the two programs. In *Tower,* the focus is not only on the building, but on the people, too. Around the time we were designing *Tower's* interface, Will saw how it could easily fit into the *SimCity* line. So I decided to develop a very "Sim-like" interface. It would become a sort of "vertical" version of *SimCity.* But anybody familiar with both games can see that the core of *SimTower* is completely different, so it is also able to stand independently.

Anyway, I guess that means Jeff Braun's representation is right on.

Barba: Tell us about the *SimTower* development process. How did you put together your Tokyo team? Where did you find people like your programmer, Tak Abe?

Saito: When I first started making *Tower,* I had no team or sponsors—no one paid attention to the idea of the game—so, I had to

be self-sufficient and provide all of the money and ideas myself. At first, I was able to develop things alone with HyperCard and paint software, designing elements such as the elevator, tenants, rules, and strategy.

But after awhile, I got stuck. I reached a point at which I could go no further without making elevator movement smoother—which is the most important part of the strategy. I also wanted the simulation to be really dynamic, so I decided I needed help.

A mutual friend introduced me to Abe. After creating a simple prototype, he suggested that we couldn't make the game without a "super computer." Because the individual people inside of *SimTower* have different personality traits, we needed a more powerful computer. Abe and I met at cafes on countless occasions. At first, the idea seemed so complicated, Abe was ready to give up. But I found some ways to simplify things.

It took a year and a half to make the graphic art, and the sound came later. My team didn't come fully together until the very end. I had worked with all of the members before on different projects, so I knew their work. From conception to marketplace, it took two years to make. I really believed in my heart that it would be a success, which is why I put so much of my own time, work, and money into it. I was very relieved when it finally did become successful!

Barba: Have you found the response to *SimTower* satisfying so far?

Saito: The response in Japan has been extremely positive—people really like it. But I'm always thinking of new features I'd like to add. I want *SimTower* to become a long-term resident on people's hard drives, just like a business application.

Barba: Are there any plans for *SimTower* updates? A "*SimTower 2000*" perhaps?

Saito: Using QuickTime, we've developed an enhanced CD-ROM version that brings the tenants to life with animation and real sound. We brought 7,000 copies to the MacWorld Expo at the end of February, and sold every one! As for a *SimTower 2,* I would like to take my time to leisurely think about it. Maybe two or three years down the line. I want to try so many different things—my head is full of ideas. I'd like to work on today's cutting edge 2-D things, but I will take my time.

More than just updating *SimTower*, I plan to create some "artificial life" products, which means the Maxis Sim Line will go in different directions. I believe it will be very exciting.

Barba: Are you looking to develop more titles that cross over between U.S. and Japanese cultures? Do you think we'll see more software titles from Japan in the U.S. market soon?

Saito: In the software world, it won't make any difference if it's Japanese-made or American-made—there is no language barrier in products like *SimTower*. Business applications have language problems, perhaps, but this game, everyone can understand.

Such games as *L-Zone* and *Gadget* (multimedia works by Japanese designer Haruhiko Shono now released in the U. S.) are wonderful products, I think. They have a great creative team, one that knows the industry well. However, I am not very interested in "Still Picture" or "Linear Movie" products. More interesting to me would be a kit that freely generates movies and pictures. I want to create a "sandbox" environment where anyone can create their own world, with as few limitations or directions as possible. That is my overall design theme.

Barba: Thanks for your time, Yoot. Anything else you'd like to add?

Saito: Yes. I'd like to express my special thanks to Will Wright, Joe Scirica, John Csicsery, George Milamn, and Michael Perry.

Index